THE LAST DAYS

Also by Charles Marsh

God's Long Summer: Stories of Faith and Civil Rights
Reclaiming Dietrich Bonhoeffer: The Promise of His Theology

THE LAST DAYS

A Son's Story of Sin and
Segregation at the Dawn of
a New South

Charles Marsh

BASIC
BOOKS

A Member of the Perseus Books Group

Published by Basic Books,
A Member of the Perseus Books Group

A CIP catalog record for this book is
available from the Library of Congress.
ISBN: 0–465–04418–2

FIRST EDITION

01 02 03 04 / 10 9 8 7 6 5 4 3 2 1

For my parents

There is a generation that are pure in their own eyes,
and yet is not washed from their filthiness.
Proverbs

Contents

1

Going Down to Laurel

One spring afternoon in 1967, when the warm Alabama air was perfumed with honeysuckle and scuppernong, my father and I were walking along a dirt path through fields of green wire grass. With his hand brushing lightly against my shoulders, he told me the Lord was calling us to Mississippi, to blessings more abundant than we could ever imagine. He assured me I'd grow fond of the new town. "You might feel a little sad for a while about leaving your friends, but that'll pass," he said. He told me my mother had cried when the final decision was made, and that was a normal reaction. But everything was going to work out just fine. My grandparents lived only an hour and a half away in Jackson, much better than the current eight-hour drive. He also told me he'd been given season tickets to the Southeastern Conference football games at Memorial Stadium, and then he promised me the bike of my dreams, a blue Stingray with flared handlebars and metallic silver banana seat. This helped make the Lord's call a lot more attractive.

Not that I wouldn't have believed him anyway. My father, Bob Marsh, was a Man of God, revered by everyone who knew him for his preaching and teaching and spiritual insight. On top of that, he was built like a linebacker and sported killer good looks. I remember once when a Sunday School teacher described Jesus to my class as being haggard and tired. I objected with indignation that left her speechless. "You are wrong about that, ma'am! Jesus had rippling muscles. He was a carpenter who banged nails in the blazing sun all day long, lifted heavy beams of wood as if they were toothpicks. There's nothin' sissylike about our Lord Jesus Christ!" I was thinking of my father.

In the late afternoons, he lifted barbells in a makeshift weight room in the garage. He wore red sweatpants even in the summer and a BAMA jersey cut off at the shoulders to expose the chiseled perfection of his biceps. He did curls, squats, jerks, and dead lifts, while I kept records in a spiral-bound notebook. He bought a bench press to improve his pectorals, adding the upper-body routine to his workout. He sweated and groaned through the pumps and presses and shouted a defiant "Hah!" when he completed a set. He strapped a piece of rubber foam around his forehead to cushion the deadweights that reinforced the muscles in his neck. When he finished in the garage, he seized the typed pages of his Sunday sermon from the kitchen table and set off on his jog.

This was the late 1960s, before jogging was cool, if not simply unremarkable. There were no running suits with the territorial slashes and waves, no spandex leggings, no scientifically designed running shoes (or if there were, you couldn't find them in the Deep South), no accoutrements of exercise that now make up the billion-dollar industry. For my father there was only a pair of low-top canvas Converses, sweatpants and jersey washed so seldom they had a life of their own, and a towel draped around his neck in a vain effort to absorb the sweat pouring from his scalp and face. I'd sometimes ride my bicycle alongside him, the two of us moving in tandem down Old Bay Springs Road, his feet pounding the pavement, beads of water shooting off his body like bullets, while he occasionally glanced down in his hands at the manuscript as he softly rehearsed the sermon.

When the day arrived, we followed the moving vans as far as Grove Hill, a town built on the eastern bluffs of the James River, and stopped for lunch at Deaver's. The three of us ate silently in the air-conditioned restaurant, my father studying the sports pages of the *Montgomery Advertiser*, my mother sipping her coffee. We had stopped before in Grove Hill on trips to see our relatives in Jackson. Today felt different. When we pulled away from the gravel parking lot in our loaded-down

Impala, crossed the one-lane suspension bridge, and headed due west on Highway 84 toward the state line, it seemed the whole world had shrunk to lonesome highway and hillside and forest. The welcome sign announced, "Mississippi: The Magnolia State." It may as well have said, "A Fallen Paradise: No Going Back."

My father's new parish, the First Baptist Church of Laurel, Mississippi, occupied an entire city block between the town's historic residential district and a small but thriving downtown. The church grounds were demarcated by 6th Avenue to the east, 7th Avenue to the west, Hudson Street to the south, and a three-acre parking lot on the north side that held several hundred automobiles. An alley ran from the middle of the parking lot through the backyards of the spacious homes lining the two avenues, connecting First Baptist with the historic district. The church owned an empty lot halfway down the alley across from the district attorney's home. There the Royal Ambassadors, a Bible club for boys, played football on Wednesday evenings with my father quarterbacking both sides, his starched white shirt soaked in sweat by game's end.

North of the church lay elegant neighborhoods with turn-of-the-century mansions intersected by worn brick streets and walkways. Most of the homes were surrounded by gardens of azaleas, English ivy, rhododendron, and Asiatic jasmine. Two blocks east of the church, the county courthouse squatted in limestone splendor, behind a tiny lawn shaded with post oaks and magnolias and a monument honoring the Confederate dead. The Pinehurst Hotel, the First Methodist Church and the First Presbyterian Church, the Busy Bee Newsstand, the

Arabian Theater, and the Manhattan Cafe formed the beginnings of Central Avenue and its dozen blocks of retail stores,
coffee shops, dinettes, and office buildings. St. John's Episcopal Church was a block off the square on cobblestoned 5th
Avenue. Designed by New York architect Frank Colby and
built in 1914, the understated Norman chapel, with the red
tile roof and terra cotta dogwood blossoms, gave locals a feeling of gentility and good breeding, even if they did tell jokes
about salvation by good taste alone and disapproved of communion wine. Knesseth Israel Synagogue maintained a declining but influential congregation a few blocks away at the
corner of 5th Avenue and 8th Street.[1] For their part, the
Catholics worshiped in a Romanesque structure flanked by a
Vatican II concrete and steel addition near the blue-collar
neighborhoods of west Laurel, marginal like the Jews, to the
downtown monopoly of Protestant power and prestige,
though everyone was polite to them.

In the late 1800s, when timberland in the Midwest was
being tapped out, mill barons looked for opportunities to set
up operations in the pine-rich regions of the South. The construction of the New Orleans and Northeastern Railroad provided such an opportunity. When the last track had been laid
in 1882, people could travel by train all the way from Boston
to New Orleans on one line. That same year, a Yankee lumberman working the dense forests eight miles north of the
hamlet of Ellisville named a new settlement for the abundance
of laurel bush growing wild. By the turn of the century, the
lumberyards of Kamper and Gardiner-Eastman (Northerners
all) had created the core of a booming and prosperous town.

The three mills that were built in the next few decades—
Gilchrist-Fordney in 1906, Wausau-Southern in 1911,
Marathon in 1914—made Laurel the sawmill capital of the
world, shipping out more yellow pine timber than any place
on the globe.

With its roots in Yankee thrift and prosperity, Laurel
seemed comfortable with its Northern progenitors, at least as
long as times were good and money abounded. Native son
James Street, whose novels *O Promised Land*, *Tap Roots*, and *Tomorrow We Reap* had been national best-sellers in the 1940s, described Laurel as "a melting pot that didn't melt, an unusual
little Southern town that had missed the blight of Reconstruc-
tion, proud of its growing pains; clean and fresh, a bit cocky."[2]
Unlike other lumber barons who disappeared when the forests
were gone, the Gardiners and the Eastmans came and stayed,
bringing along a commitment to civic flourishing and a fondness for the City Beautiful movement in vogue among urban
visionaries.[3] All parts of the city should be graceful and enjoy-
able, with plenty of green spaces, pleasing architecture, and
cultural opportunities for all.

The Lauren Rogers Museum of Art was the young town's
most impressive achievement. Lauren Eastman Rogers was the
only child of Wallace Brown Rogers and Nina Eastman and
the only grandchild of Elizabeth Gardiner and Lauren Chase
Eastman. After graduating from Princeton in 1920 with a degree in business, he married his classmate Lelia Payne Hodson
of Hoboken, New Jersey, and the couple returned to Laurel.
Rogers would assume control of the family company following a year's apprenticeship. Construction of a twelve-bedroom

estate began just weeks before the young heir died of a failed appendectomy. He was twenty-three years old.

After Lauren's death, the family authorized plans for a museum to be built in his honor on the foundations of the unfinished mansion. Rathbone deBuys, the architect of many of the original homes in Laurel and a former Princeton classmate of Rogers, was hired to design the building that would soon be praised throughout Eastern architectural circles. With an interior lobby constructed of quarter-sawn golden oak paneling and cork floors, and elegant, double-hung sash windows that opened onto an English garden, the museum was the showcase of Laurel's many architectural innovations. It was also the signature work of deBuys's Georgian revival architecture in the South. Leon Hermant, commissioned as master craftsman, used naturalistic motifs in plaster to design a vast ceiling of constellations and planets encircling a chandelier. The hand-wrought iron gates, hardware, and railings of the original museum building were created by Philadelphian Samuel Yellin. The exterior walls were made of local brick with Indiana limestone. The Laurel Machine and Foundry Company provided materials for the slender, attenuated metal columns painted cream with streamlined pillars.

When the museum was completed, the family filled the rooms with artworks from their private collection—Rembrandt, Mary Cassatt, Jean Millet, and Winslow Homer—and later purchased pieces by Jean-Baptiste Camille Corot, Louis-Edouard Dubuffe, and the Gulf Coast's Walter Anderson. There was also a large collection of Japanese woodblock prints, a half dozen European expressionist paintings, and holdings of Native American basketry featuring the museum's most popular attraction, the smallest basket in the world. Class trips to the museum always finished up around the fabulous Pomo basket, woven in the 1890s from a single blade of grass, sealed in a glass jar a quarter inch deep.

In 1926, the Browsing Room was created and furnished in a spacious addition to the main structure with floor-length tapestries, oriental rugs, and solid-oak tables. The Browsing Room—which became the city library the next year—housed the region's best collection of art history, Mississippiana, genealogy, and contemporary letters. In the early 1960s, under pressure from crusading preachers in the county, the library instituted a "red dot" policy to warn readers of fictional works containing mature subject matter. (A librarian once asked my father a little too loudly if he really wanted to check out *Couples* even though it bore the red dot.) Otherwise, the marbled halls of the library and museum paid homage to our refinement. Laurel was cultured and proud.

People in Laurel paid attention to fashion too. Back in Andalusia, our Alabama hamlet near the Florida line, most of the parishioners were hard-working country folk who made their living in meatpacking plants and bought their clothes at the factory outlet. But Laurelites traveled and patronized the arts and read John Updike and sent their children to Tulane and Vanderbilt, many miles removed from the hardscrabble South, not to mention the Snopeses and the Presleys. And New Orleans lay just two backsliding hours away, and whether you frequented the place or not, twitched on the periphery of the town's consciousness like a harlot. Interstate 55 cut right through Laurel and would carry you all the way down to sin city anytime you liked, making the possibilities of carnal excess less remote than they otherwise may have been.

My mother's new best friend flew to New York apparel marts three times a year to buy merchandise for her boutique. Before we moved, mother had ordered patterns for her dresses from the Sears and Roebuck catalog. Sometimes she bought fabric at the dollar store downtown and sewed her own outfits. But now she purchased clothes from Harper's Incorporated in the Garden Hills Shopping Center or the House of Cache downtown. She subscribed to *McCalls*, *Redbook*, and *The Ladies Home Journal* and did her best to get reacquainted with Mississippi haute couture. A *Laurel Leader-Call* article praised her appearance at a Garden Club gathering, where she wore a "multi-color tent-style dress with long full sleeves, having a fitted cuff which buttoned at the wrist." The society section routinely got more ink than all the world news put together, which comprised a below-the-fold sidebar on page two. "The ladies were served delicious punch and individual cakes along with nuts from a handsomely decorated table covered with a lace cloth and graced by a lovely arrangement of yellow gladiolus and mums combined with clusters of small white flowers." My mother took fitness classes at the YWCA and made a space in our guest room where she exercised with wrist weights, flexorcisers, hip vibrators, and black rubber stretchers. One morning a week she outfitted herself in a white tennis suit for a set or casual volley at the Mason Park courts.

My mother came to believe that if God expected our best, that meant dressing our best in addition to all the rest. "Dress right," said Clyde M. Narramore, Ed.D, in his influential book on Christian etiquette, *Secrets of Fun and Success*, which my mother, like her church friends, read and discussed. "Dress to suit the occasion. Sport clothes for outings—but dress-up clothes for church. And don't make the mistake that some do. In their effort to be 'casual' they really are just plain sloppy."[4] My mother and her church friends never made the mistake. On Sunday mornings, women moved across aqua-carpeted floors in a parade of sartorial splendor. "Savoir-faire" was the word my dad used. "Looking our best for God," was how my mother put it. Until I started sitting on the last rows of the balcony with the other kids, Sunday mornings usually meant ferocious bouts of sneezing and wheezing, as thick clouds of perfume swarmed like bees throughout the lower pews, where ladies sat with their husbands and children, looking their best in the house of the Lord.

In 1944, beneath the town and its outlying areas, beneath the rich alluvial soil of the piney woods, petroleum surveyors discovered a serpentine layer of crude oil. The Ecutta and Heidelberg oil fields instantly made Laurel the headquarters of the Jasper Wayne Petroleum Company and the location of numerous refineries. By 1957, more than a billion dollars pumped through the state economy—$32 million into Laurel pockets alone—from the 2,000 oil wells operating in Jones and neighboring counties. Everyone had a favorite story of a farmer or vacuum-cleaner salesman who had struck it rich, traded his Chevy for a Cadillac, and moved uptown. Twenty-four hours a day, seven days a week, oil wells clunked out their happy tune, on school playgrounds, in churchyards and fair grounds, and beside redbrick ranch-style homes in suburban tracts.

When we arrived in the summer of 1967, Laurel showed every sign of remaining a prosperous town. A country club had recently been built on three hundred acres of woodlands, with an Olympic pool, a golf course carved into rolling green hills by the Scotsman Seymore Dunn, and a chandeliered ball-room where smiling black men in tuxedos stood at the beck and call of club members. The Masonite plant was still going strong, belching sweet-smelling emissions from its smoke-stacks in a daily display of industrial prowess. The production of the synthetic siding was surging in response to increased national demand and a popular fascination with synthetic wood. By 1967, Masonite had a workforce of over 3,000, boosting Laurelites' purchasing income to a level $240 higher than the state's average. Laurel was a prosperous town, and First Baptist a "friendly congregation with unlimited potential" (my father said); and we worked hard to keep our happy world free of the outside forces that daily threatened the life we loved.

2

The Magnolia Jungle

We moved to Mississippi from south Alabama, where the land
was flat, like midwestern farms, wide open beneath a big sky.
The earth was red-clay or loamy, and fifty miles south sifted
into sandy soil and the shoreline of the gulf. I lived amid fields
of wire grass and scrub pines, on a country road two miles
from town, in a redbrick rancher we never locked or considered locking, and the sky enveloped the land like brilliant blue
sea.

In Laurel our house sat on an acre of land near the end of a
cul-de-sac. Dogwood and magnolia trees bloomed at the first

sign of spring, sometimes as early as February. In the oaks, Spanish moss hung like serpents around thick branches. English ivy overwhelmed the slight embankment near the street where a random row of azaleas shaped the furthermost perimeter. There was a tree house too, ten feet off the ground, buttressed by four massive pines—Mississippi pines grow tall and sturdy—covered by a tin roof and camouflaged in green vinyl.

There had never been a burglary on the street, or in the immediate neighborhood, for as long as anyone could remember. Still, our house at 8 Highland Woods, like many of the other houses in north Laurel, was equipped with security and surveillance systems—mostly self-rigged but foolproof still—to protect us from intrusion. The windows themselves were never opened, couldn't be if you wanted them to, having long been sealed shut with screws and bolts rusted now into permanence. (The central air and heating system kept us comfortable if claustrophobic.) Floodlights guarded the doorways to the house, one over the front porch that reached to the end of the sidewalk, one over the garage door (battened down at nightfall) illuminating the gravel driveway and the wooded area in the back corner (later paved over for a basketball court), and a series of sound-sensitive lights in the corner yard bordering a small creek and dense growth of pine thickets and kudzu vine. Our dog roamed the property unrestrained by fence, leash, or discipline, and at least twice a year bit a visitor or delivery man. But no one ever really complained. We were all in this together, so a canine's teeth in the calf was a small price to pay for the greater white solidarity.

Though my parents owned no firearms—a rare occurrence
in the gunslinging South—they made sure that hammers, letter openers, baseball bats, even a souvenir tomahawk I bought
in Cherokee, North Carolina, were available if needed. You
could find these hidden under mattresses or in bedside stands,
stashed away in bathroom drawers, or between panties and
hosiery in my mother's bureau. When my father was away
from town preaching in another church, my mother brought
the weapons out of hiding to rest on the nightstand. We slept
inside a locked bedroom, doors booby-trapped with bells and
tilting chairs, the house and yard outside illuminated in brilliant noon-day refulgence. I began imagining the world beyond as a menacing stranger.

In the woods behind our house, the air was damp and cool,
even in the dog days of summer, and full of strange smells—
the stagnant earth, the musk and ferns, the raw drainage trickling into a labyrinth of tiny streams. The wild vegetation was
bushhogged and macheted into submission, but still seemed
to crawl toward permeation. One earlier settler described the
region as "a wilderness, a gall-thicket among virgin timber
marching unbroken across clay hills."

I dug out a trench in the woods with the help of my friends
Bob Watts and Jimbo Daugherty—five feet deep, six feet
across in a square shape, disguised with a ceiling of moss,
mud, loose sticks, and branches. Inside we kept candles and a
bench made of sycamore roots and pieces of burlap. We
stockpiled broken bottles and jars, scraps of leather and sheet
metal, shafts of sugarcane, and whatever else we found useful.
Beneath an autumn moon we made a pact of loyalty, pierced

our fingers with jackknives, and bonded one another in blood. We marked off the compound a good hundred and fifty feet in circumference, with handkerchiefs nailed to pine trees. We moved into action at the sound of distant voices, in our brown fatigues and army helmets, with our swords of sugarcane and hickory branches whittled into arrows.

One afternoon I stood in the fort with Jimbo fixing lanterns of tin to the ceiling when I heard leaves rustle in the ground above. "Come out, you pansies, and show me what you're made of," a voice shouted to us. I seized a baseball bat, climbed the ladder as fast as I could, and stepped directly into the rusted prongs of Bob Watts's outstretched pitchfork. Bob had been late in coming to the woods and intended no harm—he only wanted to test our readiness. He'd brought the pitchfork to clear away a thorny copse nearby. For a moment, the three of us stood silently together, staring at my foot, amazed that the tool could so cleanly puncture smooth white skin between tendon and bone to bear the weight of the handle on its own.

Despite the hydrogen peroxide, iodine, and Mercurochrome—a first-aid kit was fetched from the Daughertys' house—the wounds became infected, swelling like miniature volcanoes, oozing onto bedsheets and into socks, across carpet and linoleum. But I agreed with Bob and Jimbo that it was best to keep the matter a secret, even from my parents. And so throughout the following days of infection and fever, untreated by tetanus shots or penicillin, I kept my lips sealed, determined that death was a nobler fate than betrayal, and I somehow survived. Everywhere—in the house, in the woods, on the streets of the small Southern town—I felt agitated and afraid. I later learned I had not been alone.

Since the 1954 Supreme Court decision in *Brown v. Board of Education* outlawing segregation in public schools, Mississippi had mobilized in massive resistance to the civil rights movement with an intensity unmatched anywhere else in the Jim Crow South. Ten years later, when civil rights leaders singled out Mississippi as the movement's new target, calling the state the "iceberg of southern segregation,"[1] and student activists and professional organizers began arriving from the North by the busloads in what they were calling the Summer Project of 1964, white fears reached a feverish pitch. "We are going to crack the iceberg," claimed one black activist, "and bring Mississippi to the nation."[2] White Mississippi responded by taking on a "siege mentality," described by historian John Dittmer as "so pervasive it accompanied virtually every citizen and institution."[3]

Consider, for example, the organization called Help, Inc., created in the south Mississippi town of McComb. Help, Inc. believed that black Northern militants wearing white bandannas had been handpicked by civil rights leaders to rape Southern ladies. So an extensive network of self-defense groups in middle-class neighborhoods was created to stand guard.[4] Homes were fortified with maximum care. Pistols, crossbows, shotguns, even bazookas, were mounted on bedroom walls for immediate deployment. Emergency shelters were dug into overgrown fields; police dogs were trained and sold for home protection. Help, Inc. also purchased a high-decibel sonic whistle to alert families of the coming invasion. Citizens in McComb, and soon thereafter in Laurel and the rest of the state, followed the leaders' advice to "keep inside during darkness or during periods of threat . . . know where small children are at all times . . . [and] do not sit by and let your neighbor be assaulted."[5]

The McComb organization hardly exaggerated white fears. As the civil rights movement focused on Mississippi throughout the mid-1960s, state newspapers greeted readers with a daily diet of grim news: "Anarchists on the Prowl," "Mississippi Marked for New Invasion," "The Five-Point Checklist: How to Defeat the Racial Agitators in Your Community," "Negroes Arming for Revolution: Are You Going to Sit Idly By?" We learned in these reports that Mississippi was becoming a testing ground for "communists," "Leninists," "Stalinists," "troublemakers," "beatniks," and "subversives." Photos of Stokely Carmichael shaking hands with Fidel Castro at the Conference of the Organization of Latin American Solidarity in Cuba, or of a smiling James Forman arriving in North Vietnam, appeared not only in *The White Citizen* or the *Jackson Clarion-Ledger* but also in the *New York Times* and the *Washington Post*. "We greet you as comrades because we share with you a common enemy, white western imperialist society," Carmichael was quoted as saying.

We were warned of many things: student groups, ecumenical agencies, biracial commissions, and coalitions; intellectuals and academics; journalists, poets, and bohemians. We were warned of anyone discontent with life as we knew it: the NAACP, SCLC, COFO, CORE, SNCC, the American Friends

Service Committee, the Student Peace Service Committee;
the American Civil Liberties Union, the Farmers Union, the
American Student Union, any union containing the name
"student," or any organization called "union," and all commit-
tees interested in "peace." We were warned of the Fellowship
of Reconciliation, the Methodist Federation of Social Services, the Free Southern Theater, the Mississippi Council on
Human Relations, the American Youth Congress, the Ford
Foundation, and even the National Collegiate Athletic Association, which had recently told our college teams to integrate
or face probation.

No doubt, the newspapers' dire warnings about racial
groups and peacemongers were certainly overwrought—
everyone among them Soviet agents. But they were reinforced
by no less an authority than J. Edgar Hoover, the head of the
Federal Bureau of Investigation and locally regarded as our
best defender against Moscow. Hoover's best-selling book, *A
Study on Communism*, alerted us in cool social-scientific prose to
all those devious minds "penetrating the major Negro protest
and improvement associations in an effort to exploit all controversial or potentially controversial racial issues."[6] My
grandfather displayed a copy of the book atop his writing
table next to the photos of his grandchildren—inscribed "To
Kenneth Toler, Best Wishes."

We were also warned of the cast of "Bonanza," the likes of
Pa Cartwright and Little John, especially the happy-go-lucky
Hoss, who had personally organized a last-minute boycott of
a scheduled appearance at the Mississippi Commerce and Industry Exposition, throwing in a scolding explanation as insult

to injury. "I have long since been in sympathy with the Negro struggle for total citizenship," Hoss said. "Therefore, I would find an appearance of any sort before a segregated house completely incompatible with my moral concepts—indeed repugnant."[7] The Jackson mayor called the Cartwrights' betrayal the saddest day of his life and reassured citizens that the Expo would get along just fine without them. "Jackson will be here a long time after Hoss has galloped away."[8] In fact, hold your horses, the mayor announced at a press conference, Ellie May of the "Beverly Hillbillies" has agreed to step in at the last minute. (Then, just as suddenly, the freckle-faced Clampett pulled out, pleading lack of preparation.) Unvanquished, the Chamber of Commerce took out a full-page advertisement in the paper, summoning its readers to the challenge ahead, "Let's Show 'Em Mississippi! We can produce a better show than any outside group!" Included in the ad was the new schedule of events: "Miss Jackson—Barbara Bailey—Sings; Miss Mississippi—Jan Nave—Dancing; Miss Nannette Workman—Piano and Songs; Timothy Shelby, teenage singing sensation from Taylorsville; Roy and Boots Harris and their Hilly Billy Band; 'Cito'—Nationally Famous Trained Police Dog; and Sidney Carroll Johnson—Miss Leake County of 1963—Sings and Dances."

We were warned of an African military force in cahoots with Rap Brown and Stokely Carmichael currently training in Cuba for an invasion of the Gulf Coast. Any day we would awaken to the drumbeats of mau-mau warriors packing government-supplied heat. You could find detailed accounts of these and other anti-Southern plots in *The Christian Conservative*

Communiqué, circulated throughout the state in cafés, movie theaters, newsstands, and football games and written in a steady voice. "Since 1961, large segments of the Negro population have been accumulating arms. In the event of an open armed clash, the 'Afro-American-Government-in-Exile' in Havana is prepared to put forth a major propaganda campaign for United Nations intervention. Fidel Castro is reported to have ready several hundred African Negroes undergoing guerrilla training at Marias de Frio in Oriente Province. These guerrillas will train American Negroes for partisan warfare in the South."[9] But you could also find accounts in the *Harvard Crimson,* at least the popular Jackson columnist Tom Etheridge said you could, citing from the Ivy League daily the boast of a popular student activist, "If we wanted to get a small race war going, it wouldn't be difficult. Might be a nice summer project."[10] Dark powers were conspiring against us on a massive scale.

But many Mississippians were determined not to be caught off guard. Organizations such as the white Citizens' Council vigilantly monitored the goings-on of strangers within and without. The council had been formed by a group of civic leaders in the Delta town of Indianola just two months after the 1954 *Brown v. Board* decision. By 1956, the council had eighty thousand members scattered throughout most of the state's eighty-two counties. Its members were men of the professional class, respected in local business circles, civic leaders, and church deacons. Men like my great-uncle Hilliard who lived in Kosciusko in a renovated Victorian house, drank scotch whiskey, hung his family's coat of arms over the fireplace, and traded in antiques and rare coins. The group's two main publications, *The Citizens' Council* and *The Citizen*, published a wide range of segregationist opinion—from Paul Harvey reprints to quasi-scientific accounts of black inferiority to biblical defenses of white supremacy. "The integration movement," the beloved Episcopal priest T. Robert Ingram wrote in *The Citizen*, "is one very important facet of a world-wide, highly-organized, centuries-old assault on mankind's greatest treasure—our faith in Jesus Christ."[11]

When my aunt Binky's room at the Buena Vista Hotel in Biloxi was ransacked one night during a family vacation, we feared the worst until a white serviceman from Keesler Air Force Base was arrested for breaking and entering. We were relieved enough to picnic at Ship Island the next day, but the wide expanse of gulf waters seemed an ocean of fear. The break-in had been only fair warning.

On the drive back to Laurel, my parents took stock of the situation.

"I just can't get it out of my mind," my mother said. "That man walked right by Ingrid asleep in bed in the nighttime . What if she'd waked up? What if he'd been drinking?"

"The air force will take care of him, I promise you that," my father said. "They don't mess around with this kind of nonsense."

"My precious little sister. How will she ever get over it?"

My father told us to stay in the car while we stopped for gas on the outskirts of Hattiesburg.

"I've got to go to the bathroom," I said. "I can't wait thirty more minutes."

My mother said she could wait as long as she needed. She wasn't setting foot in that awful place.

A tattooed man in a jumpsuit took my father's money and started filling up the tank. When he finished, my father pulled the Impala around to the side of the station where he could stand between the car and the bathroom. We weren't taking any chances.

3

One Preacher's Beginnings

My father began his career with a nagging stutter. He could usually get through everyday conversations without a problem. But if you put him in front of a mike, he could barely complete one sentence without the words buckling under like Pilgrim and his sack of worries. He resolved himself to conquer the demon, with God as his coach, the assistance of self-help programs he ordered through the mail, and his jogging. And conquer it he did. Mile after mile, he'd rehearse the sermons, occasionally slowing his speech to enunciate difficult words or tricky combinations until he not only could repeat the entire text in his sleep but perform it according to a catchy cadence and rhythm. In the margins of the manuscripts were cues for pausing, for gestures of the hands, the arms, and the face, or simply for charting the running time of the sermon in progress. When the Sunday morning service finally rolled around, he carried nothing with him to the pulpit but his red leather King James Bible, the kind made popular by Billy Graham, and words flowed from his lips like honey.

His parents, Howard and Elizabeth, considered him a traitor for pursuing the ministry. Whether they disapproved of his convert's zeal or were just angry he'd turned his back on them is hard to say. The sum total of Howard Marsh's piety was contained in the sign thumbtacked over the kitchen counter: "Optimism is a way of life." The last thing he needed on Sunday mornings was some showboat in a three-piece suit raining down harangues from the pulpit. Several nights a month, Howard Marsh and his fellow optimists gathered in the banquet room of the new Morrison's Cafeteria and pledged themselves to the good life. This was his church, all he needed of religion. If my father pressed him on the question of his soul's destiny, as he occasionally did—"Eternity is long, death is certain, and Dad, I must know where you stand"—Howard would snap back, "You don't have to worry about me, boy," and change the subject. He didn't intend to give an ounce of energy to organized religion, or much more to the son of his who said he wanted to preach. Howard even acted surprised when he heard the news, as if my father's decision was a betrayal he hadn't seen coming. But he was the one to blame for that.

Howard and Elizabeth Marsh had barely noticed when their son began attending the fundamentalist Youth for Christ group his senior year at Central High School. (The Youth for Christ chapter in Jackson was part of the national evangelistic organization created in 1941 and later promoted by Billy Graham.) Howard and Liz were too busy making their mark among the nouveau riche of Jackson's flourishing postwar economy. Neither could claim family prominence anywhere in their lackluster genealogies, so hopes of gracing the world of cotillions, debutante balls, and dinner parties at the country club were dispensed with early on. But they did find a comfortable spot in the shiny new world of middle-class whites who suddenly had more money than they ever dreamed possible.

Howard Marsh owned an optometry practice on Capital Street, the only one in the fast-growing downtown business and government district. Eventually he opened a second store on the first floor of a boarding house on State Street, which he expanded in the early 1960s and turned into his one citywide location, closing down the Capital Street office when the frequent sight of civil rights activities downtown became too much for him to bear. As the money rolled in, Howard and Liz did the only thing they could think of: They spent it with abandon. They added rooms to their cream-brick rancher on Buena Vista Boulevard, converting the house to a sprawling, sunny bungalow with a large playroom and back porch. They built a swimming pool and a clubhouse equipped with a green leather bar and fishnets hanging from cedar walls. They put a tropical garden around the pool, filled it with banana plants and palm trees, birds of paradise, oleander, anthurium, and calla lilies. They bought a houseboat and a dock on the Ross Barnett Reservoir, and later a ski boat and a deep-sea cruiser. They took vacations to the Florida Keys, to the Bahamas, to Cuba. And they threw parties. Cocktail hours, luaus, bridge clubs, and fish-fries. Life was nonstop Lucullan merriment around the Marsh compound.

But for my father, coming home on a Friday night after yet another basketball game unattended by his mom or dad, the sight of a party in full swing seemed the vision of hell itself. He'd disappear into his room and close the door to the den where his brother and sister sat playing hearts (the baby Scottie sleeping down the hall). He'd collapse on his bed and pray his seventeen-year-old heart out. He'd pray for his parents' salvation and the Lord's chastening hand upon them; for the wisdom to discern God's will for his life; and for the courage to sacrifice everything for the Kingdom. Prayers would sometimes heal him, loosen the tightening knot of his tongue, ease the loneliness and humiliation. And like a slow unburdening, the heaviness would lift; he'd feel clearheaded and free. If the hour had grown late and the party-goers departed, he might walk into the backyard and lie down in a lawn chair by the swimming pool, wrapping himself in a blanket if the air was cool. He'd gaze into the night sky and sense a hope so bright he'd find himself in tears. On such nights, his parents' disinterest in his life seemed nothing compared with the embracing love of God. He counted himself blessed, having been spared not only eternal damnation but also the vainglorious world of his parents.

He finally got their attention when he told them he was going to fundamentalist Bob Jones College. At first, they couldn't believe it. What had given the boy such queer notions? they wondered aloud over martinis with friends, Where had they failed? Then they got angry. Liz said she'd had enough of the hell-fire-and-brimstone business, thank you very much. She refused to put stock in a God who'd let her father get struck down by lightning. She'd seen it herself, in the spring of '26, on their homestead in the Delta, the old man Hufstadtler standing at the woodpile when a lightning bolt cracked from the sky like a whip, leaving him dead five steps from the screened porch. And if that weren't enough, the very next year the waters of the Mississippi crashed over the levee and submerged the floodplains, rolled over the house and land, and left her and her family homeless with a million others. Fourteen million acres devastated in all. For days they slept on gymnasium floors like hoboes, then later set up tents in refugee camps. They ate cold cereal on metal tables and saw everything they'd worked for disappear. No siree bob. Church might be fine on Christmas and Easter, but anything more was a waste of her time.

Howard seemed embarrassed by his son's decision. He tried to convince him to stay in Mississippi. Go to Millsaps. Go to Ole Miss. Go to Mississippi College, for crying out loud. Go anywhere but Bob Jones. But like Jesus staring down the tempter in the wilderness, my father was determined to stand his ground. So in August, he packed his trunk and hitched a ride to South Carolina.

When my father arrived on the scene in the late summer of 1950, old man Jones still ran the show himself. Bob Jones, Sr., had founded the college in 1927, after becoming tormented by the thought of impressionable young minds falling prey to the modern, atheistic, secular university. With the help of a few godly men, he bought himself some land near Okala, Florida, and built his school on the rock-solid axiom "Whatever the Bible says is so." In 1947, he purchased two hundred acres of land in Cleveland, South Carolina, and planted the school in the fertile soil of Southern fundamentalism. "The world's most unusual university" quickly flourished, adding a classical curriculum, an annual Shakespeare festival, and a course of operatic studies.

Inasmuch as "breaking the will of the child" was widely recognized as the parent's chief mission in the conservative Christian milieu of the day, Bob Jones, Sr., played the role in loco parentis with a vengeance. Dates and social outings with the opposite sex required his approval, along with the pledge to abstain from all forms of physical contact or affection (no holding hands, no hugs, no kisses, no inadvertent brushes of skin against skin, no talking to a girl without written permission, even if your paths crossed while walking to and from class, no sitting on the same sofa or chair). The dress code for girls kept skirts midcalf, shirt sleeves unrevealing, and clinging blouses and thigh-baring shorts verboten. (Hence the joke about the coed expelled for the hole in the knee of her bathing suit.) For men, it was jackets, ties, white shirts, and pressed trousers.

To enforce his discipline, Jones organized an efficient and intimidating police system. Teams of guards and investigators were dispatched daily throughout the campus grounds, scribbling in notebooks their observations of campus life, strayings from the straight and narrow, behavioral violations, and updates on investigations in progress. At the top of the surveillance hierarchy was Jones himself, dispensing demerits and spiritual warnings with an autocrat's command.

My father had never encountered anything like Bob Jones College. His Youth for Christ group in Jackson spent most of its time singing songs like "In My Heart There Sings a Melody" and "Jesus, Sweetest Name I Know," and talking about all the wonderful things God was doing in their lives. But Bob Jones, Sr., stood vigilantly against the dark impressions of the flesh and didn't care whether his students had fun or not. My father quickly became public enemy number one. He failed room inspections on a regular basis, violated the dress code, and showed up late for evening devotions. In the first month, he amassed enough demerits to get himself campused for a week, thanks in large part to his roommate—a pious Illinoisan who had won prizes for his ability to recite the entire *Epistle to the Romans* by heart—who reported him to the hall monitor at every opportunity. To make matters worse, the roommate mocked my father's Deep South drawl, called him a know-nothing and a bigot, and once taped a photograph of a lynched Negro over his desk.

My father also performed poorly in classes. "Whatever the Bible says is so" left little room for questions or clarifications. His weeklong confinement to campus was increased to a month when he lost his temper in a basketball game and slugged a player on the opposing team and the referee who intervened.

One night he reached his wit's end. He gorged himself on chicken and dumplings and washed the food down with a half gallon of milk and a pitcher of apple cider—the combined liquids having proved lethal to him in the past. He followed that with a flurry of sit-ups, jumping jacks, and push-ups. Around two in the morning, he became sick, as planned, and emptied his stomach on his roommate. Jones decided early the next day against full expulsion. This was the easy way out, not consistent with the Christian discipline he favored. A few small repairs would have to be risked before "campus shipwrecks" like Bob Marsh were thrown out as scraps. My father was hit with the maximum and permanently campused until Christmas break, which was more than a month away.

By the time Howard and Liz arrived for him at the end of the school year, he had lost thirty pounds and developed stomach ulcers. His stuttering had become chronic. Liz told him he looked like a corpse and should be ashamed of himself. (He spared her the details of his punishment for fear she might use it as one more excuse to drift farther from grace.) On the drive home, he told his parents that he was never setting foot on the Bob Jones campus again, and this pleased Howard enormously. At summer's end, Howard happily drove his son all the way to Waco, Texas, in the pounding August heat, to enroll in Baylor University. Baylor might be Baptist, but at least it didn't raise eyebrows.

4

Invisible Empires

Two miles from our church in Laurel, at the southernmost end of 4th Avenue, stood the Sambo Amusement Company, a dilapidated wood-frame building that housed a pinball machine business. There was no business sign on the building or sidewalk. The main door, a windowless slab of corrugated iron, admitted no browsers or curiosity seekers, and all the windows of the building visible from the street were boarded up. You were told to state your business on the steps outside. The eighteen-foot-high fences surrounding the building were reinforced at the top with a thick wrapping of concertina wire, as though anyone in his right mind would steal into the compound unannounced. Inside the fence a pack of underfed hound dogs scratched around the bare ground and roamed in and out of the pickups abandoned in various stages of decomposition. The Sambo Amusement Company also served as the headquarters of the White Knights of the Ku Klux Klan of Mississippi.

A man named Sam Bowers, the Klan's Imperial Wizard, lived in the backrooms of the building with his friend and business partner, Robert Larson. Bowers was something of a rare bird, as far as Klan types went. His father was a prosperous businessman, and his mother the daughter of a wealthy Louisiana planter. His grandfather, Eaton J. Bowers, Sr., had been a prominent Mississippi attorney who was admitted to the bar at the age of nineteen and served three terms in the United States Congress from 1903 until 1911. Sam Bowers took great pride in his genealogy, claiming to be a direct descendant of "the first president of the first constituted legislative assembly on this continent, the Virginia House of Burgesses."[1] He attended Central High School in Jackson in the late 1930s and lived as a teenager in a duplex on North West Street near the state capitol, a few blocks from the Belhaven neighborhood where my mother grew up. After serving as machinist mate first-class in the Pacific theater, he studied engineering at Tulane and the University of Southern California. In the late 1940s, he returned from the West Coast to Laurel, where he tried his hand in various business ventures before setting up the pinball machine company and ruling over the most violent Klan organization in history.

When we moved to Laurel in late summer 1967, Bowers had been sitting atop the FBI's most-wanted list for several years. He was suspected of plotting nine murders, seventy-five burnings of black churches, and three hundred assaults, beatings, and bombings. You'd see his face on the network news and in the pages of national magazines and major dailies, accompanied by photographs of church fires, unearthed corpses, sneering sycophants, and weeping mothers. Articles complimented his appearance: "Nattily dressed in a tan sports coat, khaki-colored trousers but without his usual sunglasses, Bowers balked at being handcuffed when taken from the FBI office to the U.S. commissioner"; "Bowers, a neat, sandy-haired man who appears younger than his years"; "the dapper Laurel vending machine company owner." He stockpiled submachine guns and ammunition in his living quarters, along with boxes of masks (large rubber caricatures of presidents, movie stars, and Negroes), manuscripts on political philosophy, racing car paraphernalia, and a wardrobe of fashionable suits and ties. One acquaintance described his habit of wearing a swastika armband and clicking his heels in front of his dog, saluting the animal with a "Heil Hitler!" He'd recently joined the Hillcrest Baptist Church, a small congregation on a country road off the city bypass, where he taught a men's Sunday School class and served as a deacon.

Bowers was a man of freakish habits no doubt. But what really puzzled federal agents was his unwillingness to change them. He didn't seem bothered by the fact that he was knee-deep in legal troubles. He was heading back to trial in October 1967 for the 1964 murders of James Chaney, Andrew

Goodman, and Michael Schwerner, the three civil rights workers killed on the first day of the Freedom Summer Project. He was under investigation for the 1966 murder of voter registration activist Vernon Dahmer. He was in and out of court for all manner of Klan-related crimes and misdemeanors. Still, he projected himself to the world with a confident smile, a swooping haircut, and boasts of a divine calling, trying hard to appear above the tedious legal details mounting daily.

Bowers had formed the White Knights in early 1964 as rumors of an upcoming civil rights invasion of Mississippi spread through the state like wildfire. A hundred thousand volunteers from Northern universities would soon be rolling across the state line in a massive assault on racial segregation, and something had to be done. (In fact, volunteers in the Summer Project numbered less than a thousand.) So on February 15, 1964, at a meeting in the town of Brookhaven—eighty-five miles from Laurel—Bowers and two hundred recruits pledged their loyalty to a new, highly secretive organization, the White Knights of the Ku Klux Klan of Mississippi, and dedicated themselves to "opposing in every honorable way the forces of Satan on earth, and in particular his agency which is called by the name of 'Communism' today." That same evening, he described the Klan's mission in his first "Executive Lecture":

> The world and all of the people in it are torn between two exactly opposite forces:
>
> 1. The Spiritual Force of Almighty God championed by our Savior, Christ Jesus.

2. The negative, materialistic force of destruction championed by Satan.

It is necessary that each and every member truly understand the above before he can ever become effective in this organization. . . . Until we all realise [sic] that we are up against a SUPER-NATURAL Force, against which our FINITE minds and emotions and abilities are, by themselves, POWERLESS to defeat, we shall continue to suffer disappointments and defeats again and again.[2]

Like his Bible hero, the prophet Elijah, who commanded the slaughter of 450 idol-worshipers at the Kishon brook, Bowers believed God had called him to purge Mississippi of the invading infidels—the "pagan academics," the "whores of the media babylon," the "degenerate clergy," all pawns in the game of the worldwide Soviet-Jewish conspiracy. Elijah Southern-style meant, for Bowers, that when the time came to kill, "it should be done with no malice, in complete silence and in the manner of a Christian act."[3] "Catch them outside the law," he advised his fellow Klansmen, "then under Mississippi law you have a right to kill them."[4]

Preferring stealth and concealment, Bowers created an environment of fear as unpredictable as the divine wrath he championed. "The Acts [of harassment] themselves should always appear to aliens as ridiculous and unimportant," he said. "Harassment itself should never aim at accomplishing any goal DIRECTLY. The purpose of harassment is to stir up and fret the enemy, then step back and wait for him to make a mistake, meanwhile preparing calmly and soberly to exploit any mistake that he does make to the maximum advantage to our-

selves."[5] He offered a list of "equipment" suitable for stirring up
and fretting the enemy: "roofing nails, sugar and molasses, fire-
crackers, snakes and lizards, mad dogs, itching powder, stink
bombs, tear gas, sling shots, marbles, BB guns, Air Rifles, bow
and arrows, and the proper use of the Telephone."[6] Crosses
might be burned on the lawns of the state's eighty-two court-
houses on the same night, even though the White Knights
were largely concentrated in no more than ten counties—
Jones County and its county seat, Laurel, being the epicenter
of the Klan's violent reign.

When my father preached his first sermon at First Baptist
and proposed to the congregation a new slogan, "The difference is worth the distance. Not the church *nearest* you but the
one *dearest* to you," Sam Bowers and the White Knights were the
last thing on his mind. Church membership had declined in the
years preceding our arrival, largely as a result of increased com-
petition and the town's northward sprawl, and this was of para-
mount concern to him and the active parishioners. "A great
challenge awaited the church," the in-house historian wrote in
her book *Our Heritage: A Foundation of Faith*. Our most visible rival
was the Highland Baptist Church, which had set up operations
near a development just across the city line on the northeast
side of town, stealing members away with the help of a school
bus that roamed the streets on Sunday morning picking up anybody with an appetite for RC Colas and hot Shipley donuts.

The "young minister with the look of an athlete" (as the
historian described my father) rallied his new staff and the
deacons into a red-dog blitz on the challenge. He filled his

calendar with breakfast meetings and lunches at the Manhattan Café, coffees and desserts at the Pinehurst Grill, suppers with church members—established, absentee, and prospective—in homes, clubs, and catfish camps. He wrote a column in the local paper and penned pamphlets and newsletters to be circulated throughout the county. He bought time on local TV and radio stations, promoting a new youth ministry with after-the-game socials and Saturday outings to the coast. He developed zone prayer meetings, with seventeen sites around town where groups of parishioners convened and mapped out strategies for church growth and evangelism. He organized outdoor evangelistic crusades, which he led himself or else teamed up on with men like James Robinson, R. G. Lee, or the flamboyant Eddie Miller. He launched dramatic advertising campaigns featuring banners draped over downtown streets, brochures dropped from helicopters during football games, and blown-up photographs of preachers and singers staked into the front yards of church members. Before revival season began, he created Brotherhood Retreats, asking the men of the church to gather for fellowship weekends at a parishioner's farm or at the public lodge on Lake Bogue Homa.

Someone wrote after a successful tent meeting in Mason Park: "It was just great. Getting outside of the walls of a comfortable building reminded members of some things they had forgotten. They remembered that it was the God of the universe they were to please. They listened to the noises of the city and remembered that out there in the night were those who needed the message, and they saw the skies in their glory and thought of Him who is the glory of life. They were re-

minded that following Jesus Christ was not easy—that to be a
Christian they had to bear a cross, not a comfortable pew."
Lest the congregation stand idly by and admire their pastor
from a distance, my father reminded them gently if not quite
patiently that the Lord's work could not be done by one man.
"Many new families are moving into Laurel," he explained.
"Find out about the ones living near you. Make personal contact with them. Have them over for coffee, ice cream, or a
cookout. Show them you care. Seek them out. Let them know
that at First Baptist there is love, interest, and Christian fellowship."

In the sanctuary of the First Baptist Church, my father
called people to reckon with the one overwhelming question,
"Are you prepared for Eternity?" "There is a life to be lived, a
Lord to be honored, a Heaven to gain, and a Hell to shun," he
liked to say, putting into perspective the all-or-nothing ur-
gency of personal salvation. He held forth against the impuri-
ties of the day, aiming his prophetic arrows at spiritual torpor,
complacency, wishy-washiness. And as was the case for Bowers and his crew, the terrain on which we marched onward was
the impalpable stuff of spiritual warfare, only our spiritual bat-
tlefield had little to do with the dreck of politics or history or
racial strife. The noises we heard were usually the wheels of
late-model autos gliding over worn brick streets, ice clinking
against crystal on summer porches, the chirping of crickets.
Bombs exploded in a separate world.

In the garage weight room, my father took a red felt
marker and copied his favorite Bible verses onto a sheet of
poster paper and taped it to the wall: "For we wrestle not

against flesh and blood, but against principalities, against the
rulers of the darkness of this world, against spiritual wickedness in high places." If you want to defeat the present darkness, you begin with the saving of souls, the renewing of
hearts, and the abiding fellowship of the congregation. And
you end there. Forget civil rights, forget social engineering.
Jesus alone is humanity's hope.

Don't get me wrong. The cross my father preached wasn't
easy. He railed against "obscenity, social perversion of morals
and ethics, immorality, and an insane desire for materialistic
gain," against "the comfortable pew," "Sunday-only saints," and
"dead religion."[7] Some preachers might be content to give
"mild-mannered sermons to a mild-mannered congregation
about how to become more mild-mannered," as he sneered
from the pulpit. Not this one. If it was your custom to grace
the church doors on Christmas and Easter—if you were on an
"empty-tomber" or one of the "manger set"—or for benefits to
career and social standing, to attract clients or customers or
make country-club connections, you could expect a good fist-
pumping harangue. "If 'church' is nothing more than a group
of people meeting to play their religious games, go through
their traditional motions, count their nickels and noses, and
serve as a sanctified mutual admiration society, then let's go
ahead and turn it into a bowling alley. At least, we've then
done something constructive with the buildings." Any hypocrite could slide in the church foyer wearing new clothes on
the Big Sundays—that didn't require conviction or commitment or intestinal fortitude. Any fool could do that. His parents could do that, wipe away the cobwebs once or twice a

year and drive to Galloway Methodist for an hour. So could
his sorry brother Tommy, somewhere off in southern California bouncing around with his third wife. So could the Devil
himself.

There is no doubt my father loathed the Klan, when he
thought about them at all. In his heart of hearts, he considered
slavery a sin, racisms like Germany's or South Africa's an of-
fense to the faith, and he taught me as much in occasional
pronouncements on Southern history over homework assign-
ments. "There is no justification for what we did to the Negro.
It was an evil thing and we were wrong." Nevertheless, the
work of the Lord lay elsewhere. "Be faithful in church attendance, for your presence can, if nothing else, show that you
are on God's side when the doors of the Church are opened,"
he advised in the church bulletin.[8] Of course, packing the
pews is one of any minister's fantasies—there's always the wish
to grow, grow, grow. But the daily installments of Mississippi
burning, the crushing poverty of the town's Negro inhabi-
tants, the rituals of white supremacy, the smell of terror pervading the streets like Masonite's stench, did not figure into
his sermons or in our dinner-table conversations or in the talk
of the church. These were, to a good Baptist preacher like
him, finally matters of politics, having little or nothing to do
with the spiritual geography of a pilgrim's journey to Paradise.
Unwanted annoyances? Yes. Sad evidences of our human fail-
ings? Certainly. But all of these would be rectified in some es-
chatalogical future—"when we all get to Heaven, what a day
of rejoicing that will be." Our spiritual energies were directed

to the deeper currents of history, the great cosmic river over-
flowing everywhere at hand, washing over worries of race and
ruin like floodwaters.

But there was more to it than that. My father had not been
convinced by the civil rights brass that God was on their side.
His one stab at commentary on the subject came in the spring
of 1965, while we were living in Alabama, in his sermon "The
Sorrow of Selma." A church parishioner who had been a state
leader in the Goldwater for President campaign nominated
the sermon for a Heritage Foundation Medal of Honor. And it
won. The medal sat proudly atop my father's desk at church—
a large bronze coin emblazoned with the words "Freedom"
and "Tradition," mounted in a wooden platform with a tiny
American flag staked alongside. He was flown to Washington,
D.C., to receive the award at a luncheon in his honor.

My father's "Sorrow of Selma" had little to do with the
hostile mob on the Petit Bridge or the killing of James Reeb,
the Boston Unitarian minister murdered the first day of the
1965 march. His sorrow was grounded in the South's dignity,
which had been stolen and mocked, in the media's portrayal of
our region "as a society of barbarians, heartless, anti-God people." My father intended to set the record straight.

> You can be an unbathed beatnik, immoral kook, sign-carrying
> degenerate, a radical revolutionary, who treats the sacred with
> disdain, and you can have no regard for decency and honesty, an
> out-and-out Marxist, an anarchist advocating the overthrow of
> everything in sight . . . and that is OK! Fine! You will then be ac-
> cepted as a broadminded liberal who represents the mainstream
> of American thought! But if you dare stand for the principles of

righteousness and morality which made this nation great, if you love individual initiative and freedom, if you think that our nation is great because it has been established within the framework of Theistic principles and must remain that way, and that the ideals of Marxism and Fabianism are dangerous . . . if this is what you believe, then the guns of public opinion are turned on you to mock you as reactionary, to brand you as antiquated, and destroy you as a member of the fanatical, radical right.

The text of the sermon was reprinted in state newspapers under the headlines "Marsh Searches Souls in Citing Selma's Sorrow." Shortly after, letters streamed in from Baptist leaders around the South, members of the Citizens' Council, John Birchers in California and Illinois. Even the honorable George C. Wallace expressed his appreciation for the words of the young preacher.

On a flight home from Atlanta, where he had preached to an old classmate's prosperous congregation in the suburbs, my father was seated behind a well-known civil rights leader and his female companion. "The man smelled like a brewery," he told us the next night at dinner. "He was lewd and obnoxious and took the Lord's name in vain. Blankety-blank this, blankety-blank that. You should have seen the way he behaved with that woman. Had his hands all over her and didn't care who saw."

When a shocking pamphlet by journalist Buck Persons appeared in print a few weeks after the Selma march, all suspicions were confirmed. "Sex and Civil Rights: The True Selma Story" offered graphic accounts of "boys and girls of both races hugging and kissing and fondling one another openly in church." Persons told of white beatniks with goatees who said they had come to Selma because they could get "'all the Negro pussy they wanted.'" He told of interracial orgies, acts of singular perversion involving beer bottles, urination, and the sparsely furnished common room at the local headquarters of the Student Nonviolent Coordinating Committee. He presented affidavits describing SNCC's executive director and a "red-haired white girl" sprawled out on a cot for everyone to see, "engaged in sexual intercourse, as well as an abnormal sex act which consisted of each of the two manipulating the other's private parts with their mouths simultaneously."[9] Not even the apostle Paul had described the depths of iniquity as unflinchingly as Buck Persons, a piercing square-jawed reporter sworn to the facts.

My father discerned in the civil rights movement and in the media's coverage of it a duplicity that preyed on the region's lost cause. "'The forget–New York and kick-Alabama club' has become the favorite pastime of a double-standard society," he said in "The Sorrow of Selma." "We are the 'bad guys,' while the demonstrators, professional agitators, beatniks, and moral degenerates are the 'good guys.'"

Although part of his indictment traded on the tired Southern fascination with Northern urban violence and the myth of our native peaceableness ("How long would I as a white Alabama minister last were I to demonstrate down the streets of New York City? How many Southerners would be in danger if 20,000 of us paraded around Chicago?"), most of his anger fell

on his two-faced colleagues in the ministry. He couldn't get
over the fact that liberal Protestant ministers, most of whom
had long since rejected the literal truth of the faith—having
dispensed with the historicity of the Resurrection in favor of
some metaphorical rendering called the Ultimate—could now
be found on a regular basis in Negro churches clapping and
singing and praising Jesus like there were no tomorrow. He offered an explanation:

> Many of these clergymen have been sent by religious orga-
> nizations of questionable credentials. This is sorrowful, because
> it points out the fact that many clergymen have nothing to
> preach in their denial of the foundations of the faith, so they
> leave their pulpits to wallow in our streets (which had been safe
> for people at night). Only the epitome of ecclesiastical arro-
> gance would compel a minister to believe he alone knows our
> situation and solutions, brazenly and blindly leave the subways,
> Central Parks, blood-bathed streets, the Harlems, the cancelled
> basketball tournaments, narcotics, political corruption, obscen-
> ity-by-the-barrels, racial gang wars, and come to "wicked old Al-
> abama" to set our house in order.

Then he turned his thoughts directly to the liberal Protestant celebrities, the likes of William Sloan Coffin and Rein-
hold Niebuhr rebuking the yahoos for their sins against
humanity:

> Clergymen, we live here, and we are deeply involved in the
> situation! Long after you have returned to your Northern par-
> adises, received your certificates of acclaim by the "scapegoat-

seeking society," and made your oratorial barbs against our "corn-pone civilization," we Alabama ministers are going to have to pick up the shambles of your sanctified rudeness, try to explain to our people why those of you who deny the deity of Christ call yourselves Christian, attempt to understand why you left your strife-torn cities and pulpits to defy law and order, goad our people into strife, and disgrace the name of Christianity. We will have deep feelings of racial tension to heal after you have smugly faded into the sunset on your way to other social revolutions.

But ranting and raving aside, my father was not your knee-jerk Goldwater reactionary. He had no interest in baptizing the Southern Way of Life or calling racial equality a "violation of God's natural law in creation," "contrary to the moral law revealed in nature," "a crime against nature," as White Citizens' Council member James P. Dees was saying in his popular essays. As a student at the Baptist seminary in New Orleans, my father had learned of his denomination's progressive views on race—views not shared by most of the pastors in our neck of the woods, but part of the public record nonetheless.

As early as 1947, the Southern Baptist convention had adopted a "Charter of Race Relations," admonishing the flock to "practice justice towards all people of all races." This meant supporting the Negro's "right to vote, to serve on juries, to receive justice in the courts, to be free from mob violence, to secure a just share of the benefits of educational and other funds, and to receive equal service for equal treatment on public carriers and conveniences."[10] In 1954, weeks after *Brown v. Board*, the Christian Life Commission adopted a resolution at the annual

SBC convention that endorsed the Supreme Court decision and called the public school system "one of the greatest factors in American history for the maintenance of democracy and our common culture."[11] The resolution was passed in a nearly unanimous vote by the 10,000 white messengers to the convention.

One afternoon during his seminary years in New Orleans, my father boarded a streetcar on Gentilly Boulevard for a ride downtown. Getting on behind him was Edwin Case, one of his New Testament professors, who walked down the aisle to the colored section and defiantly took a seat. As he passed my father, Case pointed to the "Whites Only" sign. "This is just plain stupid," he said, loud enough for everyone else to hear.

My father was quick to acknowledge that Alabama and Mississippi, like the rest of the South, had not sufficiently condemned the sins of the past, that the cause of Negro improvement should be advanced by white Christians—within acceptable limits but advanced all the same. In the "Sorrow of Selma" sermon, he warned his fellow whites that "if we do not handle the justifiable problems of racial inequality in a Christian manner, then the foes of freedom will perfidiously exploit them and the Federal government will legislate concerning them, and the manner will not be Christian." His doctoral dissertation, which he was writing at the time of the Selma march, had pondered the new social world of Paul's theology, in which "all men descended from one man, Adam."[12] Many white Southerners—not just the hard-core bigots, but the college-educated professionals as well—considered that an intolerable concession.

Still, the hard truth had to be spoken of the "proud prophets" of the civil rights movement and their "brazen arrogance." The "proud prophets" had dishonored the Gospel, cheapened the whole miraculous story with a thousand historical-critical equivocations, opting instead for a works-righteousness (at best), if not outright bravado, narcissism, moral megalomania. "Here we see hundreds of demonstrators kneeling in streets to pray; yet many of these pungent beatniks and social revolutionaries have admitted in times past that they do not believe in God, and many of these men have nothing but contempt for religion." So in the end, Martin Luther King, Jr., was a charlatan too, joining ranks with all the other social gospelers to turn the churches into "political headquarters" and "places of planned anarchy." My father concluded his award-winning sermon with a harsh indictment: "The Bible has only one word for such disgusting and crude actions—hypocrisy!"

On Sunday evenings after church, my family sometimes went to the Admiral Benbow Coffee Shop for supper. We ate in the small dining room in the back, which we reached through a cramped hallway with a short-order counter and stools. Sam Bowers spent many of his evenings here, drinking coffee and smoking with friends like Devours Nix, Charles Noble, and Travis Buckley. Alton Wayne Roberts might drive down to Laurel from Meridian or Dannie Joe Hawkins from Brandon. The Klansmen would nod politely as we walked by them toward the back room and would then giggle like adolescents when we reached our tables. I could see them through the open doorway making faces in the mirror above the grill.

The passageway to the dining room was short but terrifying. The air was thick with blue-gray cigarette smoke and always triggered my asthma. The men were aggressive and overbearing in their friendliness. Once as I walked to the candy counter, one of them spun around on his stool and put out his leg to block my way. I didn't think he'd seen me coming, but he leaned close to my face and handed me a deck of playing cards.

"Pick one, little buddy," he said.

I told him I didn't know anything about cards—which was true—and hoped he'd take that as a polite see-you-later. He and his pals roared with laughter, slapping their knees, doing 360-degree spins on the bar stools. You would have thought I'd just told the funniest joke in the world.

These were jittery fellows with fast-blinking eyes and bodies hot-wired into overdrive motion. I didn't know much at the time about what it meant to be in the Klan, since my parents never said anything about it. They were trying to protect me from the chaos outside, they later said. But I came to understand why my mother feared men like these, why she'd never stop at a gas station by herself, why she kept strangers at a vigilant distance, black and white alike.

5

The Joy of Fundamentalist Sex

My new school in Laurel was a cinder-block structure built into a hillock surrounded by scrub pines. When I joined the fourth grade in the fall of 1967, Mason Elementary was still all-white, even though the 1964 Civil Rights Act had required desegregation of all public schools receiving federal aid. In the three years since, Mississippi elected officials had constantly filed appeals and motions in hopes of forestalling the dreaded day as long as possible. But aside from a few black students attending other schools in town through the Civil Rights Act's "Freedom of Choice Plan"—the provision permitting black

families to send their children to white schools—the local
school board remained largely unaffected by federal court
mandates. Except that schools like Mason lay in a state of dis-
repair, since no one was completely sure what stood beyond
the next semester.

In my homeroom on the bottom floor, in a renovated
walk-out basement that had once been used for storage, were
two sets of doors. One opened onto a dark hallway lined with
brownish porcelain tiles and the other to the outdoor basketball court permanently dusted with a pollenous film. The
room itself was long and narrow and poorly lit. The humming
fluorescent bulbs popped on and off irregularly behind plastic
shields littered with insect parts. The low-hanging ceiling
was a collage of foul stains—yellowed rings from faulty
plumbing, monstrous patterns of mildew and mold—and arti-
facts of school life—wads of gum and coagulated peanut butter rolls.

Our desks were arranged in three rows, ten or twelve children in each. The purpose of the arrangement was to discourage horseplay by eliminating horizontal alliances of desks, but
the effect was to put those of us sitting in the back on the
fringes of audibility. We might have been less tempted to talk
among ourselves, since our immediate range of cohorts in
crime was reduced by half; but the arrangement failed to in-
spire greater learning. Part of the time I gave to staring out the
window (a motorcycle trail cut through the pine woods beyond the basketball court) or scribbling in my notebook, the
rest to figuring out what the teacher was saying.

I was especially confused by the reading exercises in the first hour of the morning. Science Research Associates (SRA) was the sinister name of the Chicago-based organization sponsoring our new reading curriculum. Innovative pedagogues had discovered a way to monitor uniformly the development of reading skills and to dispense with the clutter of books. Children would be expected to "process" and "master" a sequence of "reading packages," which came in a hierarchy of colors. Each package contained a different level of difficulty, followed by a series of multiple-choice questions. The goal was to read briskly and comprehend efficiently until we ascended to the fabulous royal blue and there was nothing left to read. River basins, cloud formations, the global migration of geese—these were the popular topics of our daily packages.

On a summer afternoon back in Alabama, alone with my father in his air-conditioned church office, I learned how to break in a new book. Folding his hands around the binding as in a gesture of prayer, my father caressed the book open until the pages fell evenly divided at the middle. He pressed the two sides with his thumbs, stretching the back tenderly to its greatest strength. He continued from the middle to both sides of the book by alternating the movement from one side to the other until the back was relaxed from beginning to end in thoroughly smooth proportions the whole way across. My father also let me help repair some tattered books he'd purchased in one of the secondhand shops in New Orleans. With newspapers spread out on his desk, we lined up a row of H. G. Wells,

Arnold Toynbee, and F. B. Meyer in worn cloth covers, and applied sprays, glues, and sealants with the care of archivists, taking delight in the magnificent glossy results.

At East Three Notch Elementary, where I attended the first three grades in the spacious rooms of an Alabama school house, I had read the entire Heroes of America biography series. But in Laurel, I never made it past remedial beige. Most of what I learned, and learned badly, was on playing fields instead. The only topic there was sex.

Jimmy Cooper's pontifications one day led me to think that babies came from rubbing penis against breasts. That evening I asked my mother about this, as I lay in the bathtub breathing mentholated steam while in the throes of an asthma attack. Does the husband put his peepee-er between his wife's bosoms, or does the woman kneel down, or squat gingerly, so the man can lean against her? Or does father hover over mother in a spiderlike sprawl?

"This is not the place," she said, touching herself lightly just beneath her breasts.

"Then what is?"

"Well, down here," she pointed vaguely, and then held her hands together decorously at the waist.

"Down where? What do you mean down there?"

My mother pointed again, a hesitant attempt to pat herself in a more precise location.

"Here in her . . . womanhood. The father swells with love . . . in her womanhood."

"What's that? What's womanhood? What's that?"

My mother was trying hard to be helpful—and I did appreciate that—but she was in over her head. Whe she started looking over her shoulder, as if she was hoping Dad would arrive with charts and diagrams, I thought, Not a chance. One earful of the discussion inside and he would have bolted straight for the weight room.

But a few days later, I discovered a book called *For Boys Only* on my bookshelf, discreetly placed between *In His Steps* and *The 50 Greatest Sports Stories of All Time*, my favorites. I immediately flipped through for illustrations and photographs and, disappointed, only then made an effort to read.

Penis between breasts actually made more sense to me than "swelling" and "womanhood." Breasts I could handle. They were something I knew about. My mother's breasts, for instance, were taut and full and completed her nice figure when brassiered, like the ads in the back of *McCall's*. But Mark Jones was my main source of information. In the spirit of late 1960s laissez-faire parenting, his mother had given him a subscription to *Playboy* for his tenth birthday (guaranteeing his status as the most popular boy in school). Mark lived on a shady dead-end street off Old Bay Springs Road in a green-shingled modern design with stone floors and skylights. He kept his magazines on a bookshelf next to the model airplanes, which I seized and studied if his mother arrived unannounced. Throughout the afternoons boys appeared at his front door concerned with the esoterica of F-1s and B-52s, and Mark politely played along.

Playboy was all about breasts in those days, with variety taking a backseat to size, as it usually does. I folded back the pages of the centerfold in anticipation of a deep-down, heartfelt stimulation, and I was never disappointed: Breasts glistened beneath a Mediterranean sun, heaved in a plush Hollywood bed, stiffened at the stroke of a Popsicle. It was like a million hissing wires jangling through my body, noises ricocheting off faraway objects like hysterical monkeys, every startling sound running like torpedoes in glorious precision. And I had to settle with *For Boys Only: The Doctor Discusses the Mysteries of Manhood*, by Frank Howard Richardson, M.D., author of the equally popular *For Girls Only: The Doctor Discusses the Mysteries of Womanhood*. In the pale light of my bedroom, blinds closed tight against the afternoon, I tried to reckon with my body's startling contretemps.

Doctor Richardson's approach to the subject combined scientific observation, pastoral evasions, and big-brotherly candor. Because he considered me "old enough to discuss things like men"—along with all my other pubescent comrades huddled over his book in thousands of evangelical homes throughout the land—I learned of the "two plum-sized glands that are contained in a bag called the scrotum, that hangs down from the crotch, just back of the penis."[1] I learned that the scrotum, or the glands housed therein, would soon enact dramatic physical changes throughout my body—like "clodhopper feet" and "overactivity of the skin glands" as well as distressing convolutions in my speaking voice. I could also expect my penis to grow, expand, become stirred in fabulous ways in accordance with exciting possibilities in the context of God's proper design, marriage.

Dr. Richardson surely meant no harm in his explanation of puberty, but the fact did not escape me that the marvels of the penis were followed by a discourse on blackheads. "Those ugly little black dots that come out when you squeeze them, followed by a little white waxy stuff" seemed to me a proper description of my emerging sexual desires, even with any working knowledge of solo-style stimulation years away. The "gradual appearance of hair on different parts of your body" and the prospects of my "organ" becoming "hard, larger and rigid"— "like the fire engine hose under high pressure"—all ran together with the oily, scaly, itchy skin, the embarrassing pimples, and sinful desires. "Squeezing blackheads sometimes causes infection, and they turn first into red bumps and then into painful boils. Your skin, that you never used to notice, may feel greasy or dry and scaly and uncomfortable; you think everybody is noticing how bad it makes you look."[2] I learned too that "long-drawn out kisses" will not in themselves cause the girl to have a baby, but they can inflame a couple "to do other things that may end up with the girl's having a baby— and most often do."

Richardson's instructions never actually described those other things, and this was the book's main flaw in my opinion. The doctor surveyed the mysteries of nocturnal emissions and the surprisingly "pleasant sensation" of handling one's own organ (I later appreciated his relative tolerance here). But when it came to intercourse, he was unequivocal and yet distressingly obscure: There was the promiscuous way, which led to the shame of a bastard child, and there was God's way, saved for that special someone in holy matrimony. "Here a man and a woman choose each other over everybody else in the whole world, just as your own father and mother did, and promise to live together and make a home for themselves and the children they may bring into the world. This is the natural way, the purpose for which sex was provided."[3] But no light was shed on what the natural way was all about. I'm sure the last thing Dr. Richardson and his editors at the Sunday School Board wanted was an instructional manual for horny fundamentalist boys, but I could have used some of the basic one-two-threes, if only to calm my nerves.

After I had gleaned what wisdom I could from the good Dr. Richardson, some more information on Christian sex appeared in my room. This time it was a sermon on cassette by a preacher named David Wilkerson. The sermon was called "Parking at the Gates of Hell." David Wilkerson would become one of my heroes—one of every good Baptist boy's heroes—the Bible-wielding evangelist who traded his Pennsylvania suburb for a rathole in Hell's Kitchen and confronted hoodlums and junkies in the name of Jesus. I read *The Cross and the Switchblade* several times by the time I was thirteen, and could have easily answered multiple-choice questions on gang behavior and drug paraphernalia. Pat Boone starred as David Wilkerson in the motion picture release, which played for months at the Arabian Theatre in downtown Laurel thanks to the patronage of every youth group in Jones County. "I am just a country preacher," Wilkerson announced to the "hooting, catcalling mob," the rivaling Hispanic and Negro gang-bangers, "but I have a message for you."

Eric Estrada, in a pre-"Chips" leading role, was cast as Nicky Cruz, the baddest blood in town. "Go to hell, preacher," Nicky sneered. "If you come near me, I'll kill you." But Nicky's threats were no match for the prophet from Pennsylvania. "You can cut me up in a thousand pieces," Boone replied, "lay them out in the street, and every piece will love you." Nicky dropped to his knees and surrendered his life to Jesus in the movie's final minutes. Gone were the days of riot and rumble. There wasn't a dry eye in the house.

Nicky went on to fundamentalist fame on the heels of his conversion and his own memoir, *Run Baby Run: The Explosive True Story of a Savage Street Fighter* (over 2 million copies sold), which I read with an even greater appreciation for God's grace and the vicarious thrill of rebellion. Wilkerson hit the circuit, too, seizing upon his reputation as a fearless evangelist and founder of Times Square Chapel Ministries (and author of the book that would sell 12 million copies) to speak to other issues that moved him. He predicted the end of the world in 1978, and then again in 1984. In 1985, with the earth still spinning in its orbit, he likened America's "wild, roving mobs of homosexual men" and "filthy perverts" to "one great holocaust party, with millions drunk, shaking their fist at God, daring him to send the bombs."[4] "Sudden destruction is coming," and few will escape. Had the apostle Paul let the fornicating Romans off the hook just because they were too gone to care? "Unexpectedly, and in one hour," said Wilkerson, "a hydrogen

holocaust will engulf America—and this nation will be no
more. . . . It will all be gone! The stock market will burn—
with all the buildings, the investments. The skyscrapers will
melt; the fire of divine vengeance will turn cities into polluted
wildernesses. . . . Make no mistake about it. God's word
clearly warns a great dissolving will happen."[5]

I never saw Wilkerson preach a crusade, but I could tell
from listening to the cassette that you would leave a changed
man. At least, you wouldn't be caught parking with a girl for
many a moon. I listened to screams of agony, Lucifer's flames
dancing their eternal mocking lambada, tormenting without
consuming the endless sea of erotic bodies, all because of the
parking and the petting—not just the beginning of the slippery slope to premarital sex but the veritable avalanche to the
gates of Hell itself. I listened to wails of regret and remorse—
"If only I'd saved myself; if only I'd waited; if only I'd kept myself pure!"—but the time of decision had passed, lust and
desire fueled now everlastingly in Hell's fury.

I wasn't even sure what went on in parked cars. I thought
of petting as an affectionate gesture to dogs and cats, and
heavy petting as a somehow heavier version of the same, but
when applied to humans, hence the perversion. Still, I imagined Hell as a place of unconstrained desire, where teenagers
chained to lust in a tragic fate had swapped a moment's pleasure for an eternity of torment without so much as a second
thought. Parking must be awesome, I thought, and avoided at
all costs. Imagine it: the moaning and groaning and the pitiful
little bastards!

What followed next was a long procession of youth
speakers, men from the Campus Crusade for Christ, from the
Navigators, from start-up ministries in Starkville and
Tuscaloosa, all of whom "related" to teens and had "dynamic"
testimonies. They wanted us to surrender our hearts to Jesus,
to reckon with our "total depravity," to turn our sights from
worldly distractions, and seek a pure heart. They wanted us
to receive Jesus Christ as our personal Lord and Savior, to become born again to travel to the "frantic center of the spiritual life."[6]

I'd hear the youth speakers at Sunday evening services
(more informal than the eleven a.m.), fellowships after the
football game in parishioners' homes, skating rink crusades
(temporarily cleared of skaters), citywide rallies in the stadium
or tent meetings in Mason Park. They rarely failed to relate,
these fellows in their white cotton trousers and pullovers, with
their smooth southern California wits. They talked about their
lives b.c. (before Christ), how God had tracked them down in
unlikely places, about strategies of effective evangelism—
nothing better than "The Four Spiritual Laws" tract—and
about keys to a winning quiet time. But mostly they talked
about sex and drugs.

A dynamic testimony meant you were in for a treat. My favorite was Josh Seargrove's.

Josh was from Houston, Texas, and had been raised in a
Christian home. He'd attended a Baptist church with a Bible-
believing preacher and made a profession of faith as a ten-
year-old boy. His parents were loving and godly. They'd

done everything to raise him right, but something had gone wrong. He'd rebelled, fallen into a bad crowd, and "yoked himself unequally with unbelievers." After that it was only a matter of time before he tried drugs, pot being the first link in the drowning chain, smoking it as often as he could, accompanied by the music of Ravi Shankar and Bob Dylan, his body rising and sinking to the meandering rhythms in some friend's basement hideaway. He had fun with pot, no doubt about it. "The Devil's playground has its pleasures—why do you think so many people play there?" But Josh soon craved a higher high and moved on to LSD and mushrooms, listening to Jefferson Airplane and Cream, soothed now in psychedelic caress by the black-light posters that covered his ceiling.

Josh was now caught in a "cycle of diminishing returns," meaning that the lows got lower and the highs higher, meaning that once you give Satan an inch he'll take a mile and you'll soon become his slave. Josh needed more to fill the hole in his eighteen-year-old heart, and heroin proved just the thing, snorted, smoked, or injected while listening now to the chants of the Devil worshipers who shared his pied-à-terre in the French Quarter. (All of this was re-created with graphic precision for the gasping audience.) Josh ended up in New Orleans, because that was the only real option for a white boy from Houston hooked on smack and in love with a witch. He made handbaskets and sold them on the streets. He read Nietzsche and Buddhist philosophy in Jackson Square. He sat by the river and smoked cigarettes.

Actually, he had fallen in lust with the witch, he told us, not in love, and they petted heavily and had premarital sex, and sometimes even had sex with other witches (and warlocks!) all together at the same time.

"I was searching," Josh said after a dramatic pause. "I was lost and I was dying and I was searching for truth."

Truth arrived one fair morning in the form of his father and Josh's best friend, a pair of handcuffs, and twenty feet of Texas-quality rope. His parents had tired of letters returned to sender and phones hung up in their faces. So with the help of Jim Langley, himself just off drugs and gladly summoned into action, Josh's father planned his mission of mercy. Arriving in New Orleans before the sunrise, the two men sat in their car at the corner of Bourbon Street and Esplanade sharing a thermos of coffee. They waited patiently throughout the early hours of the day, praying for strength and a miracle, telling stories of prodigal sons restored to life, singing songs like "Amazing Grace" and "Victory in Jesus," until finally the doors swung open across the street and Josh emerged squinting in the midmorning sun. Before he had a chance to sweep back his curly blond hair and put on his sunglasses, he was apprehended, handcuffed, roped and tied, and thrown into the backseat of the car.

"I was on my way to score, but God got me first."

That night, after much obscene foaming of the mouth on the long drive home, Josh stood beneath a hot shower in his parents' house and heard the words spoken aloud, "I am calling you according to my purpose." Josh fell to his knees, sobbing, broken, penitent, the heavy burden of addiction sliding off his back, without withdrawal, without the urge to shoot up. Josh was born again.

"And you can be, too, young person," he explained, tears glistening in his baby-blue eyes. "You can be healed of the sins that torment you, whatever they may be. You can be forgiven."

Here was the rub: I lacked a dynamic testimony. At youth nights or around campfires on retreats, I had tried to relate tales of my own wickedness, but there wasn't much to work with. I'd once watched Bob Watts drink a beer in my backyard, so I could try to say a word about the wild friends who kept me down. But I'd also slugged him in the head in righteous anger and sent the can flying—an act that no doubt pleased God but did nothing for my testimony. Part of me wanted what Josh had: a journey to God with an extended layover in New Orleans. But part of me felt betrayed. You blow your yah-yahs out, get Jesus, and settle down to a good life. Isn't that what the dynamic testimony was all about? It seemed kind of unfair, really, forgiveness pouring over the wretched and virtuous alike. Rebellion ultimately belonged to the rebellious, I concluded. But I was aimed toward purity like some overeager bird dog, sniffing out every thicket and underbrush.

"If you want to be a winner, you must live according to God's rule." This was found in *Patterns for Christian Youth*, which assumed a place of honor in my parent's sacred canon, alongside the Bible, Amy Carmichael, and *Street and Smith's College Annual Football Roundup*. But to my young mind, God's rules seemed a lot more flexible than theirs. The prodigal son hitchhikes to the Big Easy for a nonstop feast of debauchery, then crawls home jaded but forgiven. Grace works a lot like that, at least in the Bible's earthy accounts of forgiveness and embrace. But in my little world. I watched the action from a distance, a Man of God in Progress, hoping to some day become a winner, and doing my best to play by the rules.

The writer Lillian Smith once described the religion of her Southern childhood as one "triangulated on sin, sex and segregation."[7] There was a God in heaven who loved the world and gave his son as a sacrifice for its sins; but this same God would cast into the Lake of Fire anyone who dishonored him. There were parts of the body that must be separated from curiosity and touch, honored but feared. Segregation was "a logical extension" of the lessons on the erotic body and the inscrutable God. "The banning of people and books and ideas did not appear more shocking than the banning of our wishes which we learned so early to send to the Darktown of our unconscious."[8] Aspirations to personal holiness marked the South's heralded piety, its devout and feverish mind.

Then there was a different twist on the same notion. God loves us so much he might hurt us—"Behold, I have chosen thee in the furnace of affliction," God tells the prophet Isaiah—through trials and tribulations, through the dark nights of the soul, and through our region's tragic memory. God sometimes puts us to the test, casts us into the refining fires of his love in order to make us "more precious than gold." "People, like God and parents, can love you and hate you at the same time," Smith wrote, "and though they may love you, if you displease them they may do you great injury; hence being loved by them does not give you protection from being harmed by them."[9]

The problem was that you couldn't quite know what to expect. For example, there was the case of the Unpardonable Sin, or sinning against the Holy Spirit. Jesus explained: "Wherefore I say unto you, all manner of sin and blasphemy shall be forgiven unto men: but the blasphemy against the Holy Spirit shall not be forgiven" (Matthew 12:31). I couldn't believe my ears the first time I heard it. Here was Jesus, the same turn-your-other-cheek, blessed-are-the-merciful Jesus, showing us the dark hole in his big love. All sins would be forgiven but one. And he wasn't saying which.

I was trying like crazy to figure it out. My Man of God in Progress books were starting to outnumber the sports and the classics. And the picture was starting to come into focus. "The most wonderful gift you can give your future bride or groom is your purity."[10] "You see, not only the minds, but the bodies of Christians are a sacred trust. Having been cleansed by Christ, they should be kept clean for Christ. And to permit them to be used to 'paw' over, or to be 'pawed' over, is to follow the diabolical suggestion of hell itself."[11] "How wicked to debase ourselves and defile our bodies in unholy lust, deliberately inflaming sex passions like whoremongers and harlots."[12] "Don't fall into Satan's trap and sell your soul for a shameful experience that will haunt you as long as you live."[13] "Strip tease and leg shows, bathing suits which unduly expose the body, particularly women's bodies, magazine stories and pictures that turn the mind especially toward love-making, the movies, the embrace of the dance—these lead to sex desire and so to necking and petting."[14] "God wants more than just a person's mind or his service in some future career. He wants one's body. Now! When a young person presents his body to God, the Holy Spirit comes to live in him. His body becomes God's home which must be kept pure and clean for Him!"[15] "The constant arousing of desire may result in self-abuse, causing guilty consciences or even nervous breakdowns sometimes. With men there is often a serious loss of semen which depletes the physical strength and sometimes affects the mind."[16]

"You need Jesus Christ to give you strength in (1) purity (2) dedication (3) courage," my parents wrote in a birthday letter. As further incentive for the journey ahead, my mother, assuming an air of clinical detachment, explained to me that premarital sex leads to psychic ruin. "All the girls I know who've lost their purity have emotional scars. Their thinking is somehow damaged. They've lost a precious something they can never get back. Their personalities are distorted, become one with that other personality." They'd committed the Unpardonable Sin. Not that my mother understood it this way. It just seemed the logical conclusion to draw. I imagined unceasing despair, the snapping of synapses, normal bodily functions collapsing all around. I vowed not to touch the stuff.

Still, I'm not sure what she was responding to. Christian books and manuals were no doubt fodder for her view, with their descriptions of "havoc in the psychological life" and "the mental imbalance wrought by promiscuity." But this didn't seem true of the wild kids I'd heard about. Like some of my mother's Sunday School girls who were forward and loose, they got through their days just fine, woke up, ate their grits, showered and shaved, and in other ways functioned just fine as far as I could tell.

Mother occasionally mentioned the subject of "complete nervous breakdowns." Once you got one you'd never be the same. Old parson Barnstorm had had one. He'd pastored the church a decade earlier. He now lived in the back rooms of his home on Maple Street where his wife taught me music lessons. Each week, I heard him thumping around his quarters, sometimes letting out a wild staccato bark so loud it startled us on the other side of the house. Garth Blount's uncle Frank had had one, too, during his freshman year at Cornell. Garth was one of my best friends, a melancholy boy who lost his dad in Vietnam and later became a plastic surgeon in Hollywood. Uncle Frank lived in private rooms in the back of the Blounts' rambling Victorian home on 16th Street. Frank had once shown all the promise in the world—a brilliant young mind, good looks, a friendly disposition—but the Ithaca winters had taken their toll. When Garth and I played APBA football in the den, we could hear the man talking to his television set. Sometimes I spied Frank making one of his occasional forays into the kitchen, dressed in his soiled boxers and red Cornell sweatshirt, a smile stamped on his face. Most folks said he'd succumbed to bad genes and mania, and to all the weird books his philosophy professors had assigned. But I knew better. I knew Uncle Frank had gotten in trouble with sex, messed up his purity and then his mind.

I opted for a simple intimacy, no probing and sticking and plunging of things, but a touch, though not even a touch really, just a slight hesitant rubbing of skin on skin, as if I might find thereabouts a space where desires roamed holy and pure. I'd memorized the apostle Paul's advice about presenting your body as a living sacrifice to God, not being "conformed to this world," being "transformed by the renewing of your mind." In the margins of my black leather *Thompson Chain-Reference Bible* (King James Version), alongside the *Epistle to Romans,* was printed a list of related topics with verses adjoining: "spiritual darkness," "revelry," "drunkenness," "lasciviousness," "wanton-ness," "flesh," "lust." From here you were directed to chain refer-ences (numbers 3193–3221) in the study guide for the appropriate remedy: "Self-Abasement," "The Follow of Self-Ex-altation," "Self-Examination," "Subduing the Flesh," "Restrain-ing the Appetites," "The Duty of Self-Denial," and "The Renunciation of All Things for Christ." Perpendicular to the list, in the furthermost right margin, I added my own heading, "Dead to Sinful Things," underlining "Dead" with a red felt pen.

I had carefully inscribed "The Four Spiritual Laws" in the back of my Bible, the soul-winning method popularized by the Campus Crusade for Christ. The fourth and final law fea-tured two circles illustrating "the two kinds of lives available to man." A stick shape in the middle of each represented a throne—the throne of a person's life. Whatever occupies your throne, Ego or Jesus—"E" or "T" †—controls your life, your values, your priorities, who you date, who your friends are, the books you read, the movies you see, the music you listen to, *the Master you serve.*

In my little kingdom, I wanted Jesus on the throne and ego exiled. I wanted "the fullness of Jesus" in me. But there were times, too, increasing in frequency and intensity, when my muscles felt ornamented with the tails of savage animals, dancing to the accompaniment of sticks and bones. That I checked out Mark Jones's model airplane collection on a regular basis was one sure sign of my losing battle with "E." "Garbage in, garbage out," my father preached. "What your mind takes in, your actions give back. Junky thoughts in, sinful actions out."

One morning on the playground, Larry Frazier unfolded a pornographic picture from his wallet and passed it around the basketball court. All I could figure was a soupy labyrinth of okra spears and woody knots angling over a blond stew. My classmates and I huddled over the photo with the concentration of brain surgeons, mouths agape and the occasional belly-moan of comprehension. Some of the boys seemed eager to jump right in. But comprehending little, I stood speechless, the first simple man catching sight of the Wholly Other, full of tumult and the thrill of revulsion, stupid and aroused.

I knew my body was the temple of the Holy Spirit. I must remain pure until I met that Special Someone. But the more I learned of my contemptuous flesh, the less I remained content with my innocence. The gritty fact of my depravity might have felt exhilarating, had it not weighed down like a summer storm, accompanying my every thought and movement like a dull, heavy ache. In time, too, I deployed a set of contingency plans to keep desires in line, or at least unnoticed. Never volunteer for math problems on the blackboard in the languid hours after lunch. Keep the blazer buttoned during Sunday

School. A jockstrap might even be donned as a protection against erections. They felt so good, they had to be sinful.

One of my father's favorite books was *Pilgrim's Progress*, which he read to me from an oversized children's edition that had Daliesque illustrations. I witnessed stalwart Christian embark on his journey, the pagan sun spreading its dull light over the land, vices bundled in burlap, strapped to his back, legs straining, muscles burning, everybody wishing him ill. I visited Vanity Fair, a psychedelic dread of confusion, where lewd peasants in filthy rooms gorged, groped, fornicated, farted, the foul remains of the Old Man. I visited the long, long road, the winter evenings settling down, the shadows stealing across the sky, and then the pearly gates, the burden removed, the crossing over, Payday averted, God be praised. I made the obligatory trek down Romans Road. "For what I do is not the good I want to do; no, the evil I do not want to do—this I keep doing."

I really would like an ice-cream sandwich, I think to myself one summer morning, as I hear the bells of the ice-cream truck signal its arrival. But I'm so excited I scream, "Ham sandwich! Ham sandwich!" and the driver puts pedal to metal, as I give lunatic chase to the end of the street. "I have sinned. I have gone astray," reads an entry in my first spiritual journal. "Sin brings death. Damnation." I draw a picture: A boy is running across an arid plain toward the gray horizon. "I cannot earn my salvation." I am a lost sheep gone astray. "What must I do?" I write. "Who can save me from the wretch I am?"

Now it's nine-thirty, Sunday morning. I'm sitting in the cold metal chair in the opening assembly of Sunday School in the throes of arousal. My sights have drifted to the legs of Callie-Ann Berkshire, exposed up to the pink trim of her panties thanks to the precipitous curve of the folding chair. Before me sits an entire row of girls, cross-legged, supple, deep-thighed, and silky. I look away. I search my brain for help. "Whatsoever things are true, whatsoever things are honest, whatsoever things are just, whatsoever things are pure, etc., think on these things." I try to think of something pure. A blue sea on a summer day. A blue sea filled with girls in bikinis. Think again. A baseball game. I'm batting cleanup. The score is tied, bottom of the ninth. I hit the ball out of the park. The girls in the cutoff jeans shriek with delight. My thoughts go down the tube. I think of Jesus. The suffering, bleeding body. His sufferings poured out for me, arms stretched in agony, saving me from ruin, the oblivion. Callie-Ann puts her legs together—thank you, Lord!—but then (No! No! YES!) her underwear, the color of ripe peaches, glows between her thighs like the blooming of love itself.

Identify with Jesus, his torment, his anguish! And don't forget. He's coming again soon, and it won't be pretty. Think on these things. I try, oh God I try. But prohibitions collide with admonitions in a train wreck of desire: Never mind the Atonement, the vicariousness of the Cross, Jesus suffering for the sins of the world. I work the wretched logic through the knottiness of my will and reach a different shore. I become the suffering Jesus, welcome his torments and agony, in recompense for all I am and should be.

I would not later abandon the straight and narrow in my adolescence. I never ran off to New Orleans for a little well-deserved excess. I found tolerable limits, half steps, the roaming finger, whatever, but I never really thought I would go all the way. I believed Jesus would return to enrapture his church before I had the chance. Or maybe I'd be left behind anyway just for thinking about it, a virgin and mad as hell. And the prospects of picking up then where I left off were not good, as I surmised in my journal: "The Great Tribulation—earthquakes, hailstorms, 110-pound chunks of ice, sun will go dark, moon will not shine." But I needn't really worry about the seven years of misery. My body handed out punishments like an angry god, and would only get better over time.

6

Fun and Success in the Closed Society

High school girls came to see my mother in the afternoons. Most of them were members of her Sunday School class. She offered them spice tea and a shrink's confidence, and they told her secrets they'd never tell their parents. My mother had "the gift of discernment," my father told me. "She can see into your deepest thoughts. The girls feel free to open up with her. I've never seen anything like it. She has a real gift, and you should be proud."

Sometimes I listened from the other side of the kitchen door. I'd hear the confessions of a girl whose purity had been lost, her quiet sobs, and my mother's consolations. I'd hear of girls flirting with disaster, testing the limits of desire, of brutal lust and molestation. I'd hear stories of sex in numbers, of girls needing it like oxygen, of some who'd spread their legs for the glory of the Lord. One Watkins High cheerleader annotated her *Scofield Reference Bible* in a hermeneutics of carnal pleasure, teasing out a seducing phrase or line where possible—"Let my beloved come into his garden and eat his pleasant fruits"—any insinuation to indulge the body's grace. And always my mother's gentle assurance, her admonitions toward a more disciplined faith—her praise of purity—though she did not condemn the girls, and they did not feel condemned. If anyone deserved blame, it was the parents, my mother would tell us later, their lack of Christian priorities, their conformity to the flesh, their concern for society.

Josh Seargrove's mom and dad no doubt harbored secret resentments and hang-ups. "Something had gone wrong at home," my mother explained to me at dinner one night. "Something wasn't quite right." When a teenager rebelled, it was rebellion against the parents (and God, of course, though more abstractly). The parents had failed to raise a child pleasing unto the Lord. In Josh's case, she didn't know exactly what that was, but in plenty of others she knew the full scoop.

Suzie Hightower was an example. Suzie had felt another girl's genitals on a sleep-over at a friend's house and not only enjoyed it, along with the reciprocated touch and whatever else followed, but had come to crave the bodies of women, their tastes and smells—it all turned her on. Suzie sat at the kitchen table, smoking her cigarettes one after the other, offering her information not as a confession but as a statement of fact. She was "in rebellion," as my mother would put it, she made no apologies. "In rebellion," ordinary rules were suspended, my mother believed, and she would listen patiently, consoling and praying, and again not saying too much and trying not to judge.

Only later in the evening, when we were eating supper or watching television, would she explain. Orin Hightower, Suzie's father, and Parcelle, her mother, did not show proper affection among themselves or their children. They were country people who didn't understand the complexities of child-rearing. Lacking proper affection could also signal sexual problems. At least, "something had gone wrong" always struck me this way, though no specifics were given. I got the impression that the parents just didn't get enough between them, that the flames of passion had waned or spread elsewhere. Thus, as I understood it, my mother seemed to imply that not only could too much sex too soon ruin you, but too little sex too late as well. How to know just how much and when seemed one of those mysteries that continued to elude me. Mother seemed vindicated by the daily feast of erotic misadventures, by the widening panorama of parental failure in contrast to the tight ship she ran.

My mother blamed a lot of these things on society. She might say of Neill Gardiner, one of Laurel's few authentic grandes dames, "she's old society," and by that mean, if not an outright compliment, at least a plain acknowledgment of the proper order of things. The Gardiners' patronage of art and

opera—they discovered Leontyne Price's exquisite voice—
and garden parties where "wine flowed freely" (my mother
sighed) might even be appreciated for what they were, privi-
leges of a storied family. But then she would say of a woman
like Marlie Jacks, our buxom neighbor whose pudgy husband
owned a booming chain of dollar stores, "she's just society,"
and mean, "she's trying to be old money but doesn't have a
chance." (A polite way of saying "she's kind of slutty.")

"She's just society," or even "she's society" or "they're society," actually contained two serious charges: compromising
Christian principles and the disgrace of tackiness. Tackiness
involved trying to be something you weren't and couldn't be
in a million years. "That's a big house, isn't it, and they grew
up country." Compromise meant selling the Lord short, and
by extension the church and all those who do its work (especially my mother and father).

In fact, my mother came to the subject with an advantage
few pastors' wives could claim. Before she married, she moved
for a time in Jackson social circles, only later to shun them.
Her advantage also contained an embarrassing little secret:
She had been admitted into Jackson society because she could
charm the horns off a billy goat. The circles she graced were
not really hers by entitlement. Her father, Kenneth Toler, was
a twice-married Cajun who worked for an out-of-town newspaper, where he had a reputation as an honest reporter with an
independent mind.

Her mother, Lillian Haegstrom Toler, was the daughter of
a Swedish immigrant who'd lived in Michigan before settling
in Lumberton, Mississippi, where he spent nearly two decades

in and out of sanatoriums, promising his wife and children he'd give up drink, until he turned a shotgun on himself one sad winter afternoon in 1924. I was always secretly pleased with this strange intermingling of melancholy Swedes and Acadian Catholics, but it didn't add up to much in the Southern social register of 1953.

The Toler family lived in Jackson in a small English Tudor home on Fairview Avenue, between Belhaven and Millsaps colleges. This was not a bad place to live if you wanted to mingle with the movers and shakers and powerful players of Mississippi life. Belhaven was a neighborhood with wide streets and sprawling oak trees, and a fantastic mix of architectural styles: an antebellum home next to a Spanish stucco design; a renovated shotgun house next to an experimental enclave of stone, steel, and glass. Ross Barnett lived across the street, and though most of his neighbors considered him an ignoramus, proximity to the powerful attorney and hard-breathing segregationist (soon to be governor) counted for something. William Simmons, the Virginia-educated attorney who presided over the Citizens' Council with a dandyish flair, occupied his family's estate on the lush summit where Fairview intersected North State. Eudora Welty lived around the corner on Pinehurst Street, a stone's throw from Belhaven College, and gave the neighbors a pleasing but unfathomable sense of their literary privilege. My grandmother might even boast of her acquaintance with the writer if she were staying at the Peabody Hotel in Memphis, although with close friends she'd tell you there wasn't much difference between Welty and Faulkner when it came to making white people look bad. Anyway, why hadn't Eudora ever gotten married—this was the nagging question on the neighborhood ladies' minds. (Lonely Mrs. Pippen around the corner got married, but annulled it when her husband turned out to be impotent.)

My mother was smart and fun and thoroughly at home at Central High. She edited the *Cotton Bowl* yearbook and led the HI-Y group on Tuesday nights. She gave herself to her friends and classmates generously, with an almost aggressive desire to solidify their trust. Protestant and Catholic, Gentile and Jew—everyone reciprocated her kindness. "The good Lord made all kinds of people but there haven't been any made yet that could stand up to you. You're the absolute tops in everything," her escort to the senior prom wrote in her annual. Myra Toler was the epitome of Southern charm. "Your friendly ways and constant smile will stay in my memory forever. When the world goes bad and gloomy, I know you will be looking at the good side of life. The fellow that captures your heart will get a very rare jewel." "The beauty of Myra's face speaks out the modesty and humility of her mind. Her outward loveliness is the soul shining through its crystalline covering. We shall always consider her friendship an exquisite treasure, for it is without a falsehood and is built on sincerity as constant as the North Star." By the time she graduated in the spring of 1953, she had racked up all those school honors pertaining to the pretty, the perky, and the promising: Most Friendly, Most Versatile, Miss Central High of 1953, and valedictorian of the senior class.

She had also come to love the Presbyterian church and the crisp doctrine of the Reformed tradition. She could expound lengthily on the *Westminster Confession*—having memorized the *Shorter Catechism* by the age of ten and read the *Institutes of the Christian Religion* by the time she finished Central High. Calvinism proved irresistible to genteel Southern tastes, with its clean and tidy take on life, its reliable rhythms and closures, its depiction of human lives and histories mapped out before the creation of time, the whole great expanse of creation brought under God's perfect dominion. "What is the chief end of man?" reads the *Shorter Catechism's* first question. "Man's chief end is to glorify God and to enjoy him for ever."

My mother felt a compulsion to learn more. She turned down the scholarship to Ole Miss (hers as valedictorian) and began theological studies at the Presbyterian school down the street. She continued to live in the house on Fairview, keeping her bedroom with the lavender wallpaper and the four-poster bed she shared with a sister. But at Belhaven College, she entered a new world of ideas, and she soon made it her own.

Belhaven's president at the time was a kindly segregationist named G. T. Gillespie, who distrusted Shakespeare because he couldn't get a handle on his religious views and who had only recently allowed a little Faulkner into the curriculum.[1] His twice-weekly chapel service (required of all) offered gentlemanly expositions on Scripture with an eye toward refinement and manners. Gillespie's pamphlet, "A Christian View of Segregation," would soon become a widely revered manifesto of white Christian resistance in the South, with its lumbering commentary on the "current race issue" amounting to "the

choice between the Anglo-Saxon ideal of racial integrity
maintained by a consistent application of the principle of segregation, and the Communist goal of amalgamation, implemented by the wiping out of all distinctions and the fostering
of the most intimate contact between the races in all the relations of life."[2] But in the fall of 1953, in those final days before
the Supreme Court's treachery, his real interest lay in the well-
being of the four hundred girls he treated as the daughters he
never had.[3]

Gillespie made sure his students learned their Reformed
theology, not the etherealized Anglicanism of Hollins and
Randolph-Macon or the transcendentalist vagaries of the New
England schools. Theology was still queen of the sciences at
Belhaven, and to his credit, Gillespie would not settle for sec-
ond-best when it came to picking his faculty. He hired men
from Edinburgh and Philadelphia and Amsterdam, well versed
in classical studies, fluent in Hebrew and Koine Greek, committed to the Reformed principle of *sola scriptura*. And the Belhaven theologians did not let him down. They attacked
liberalism with minds quickened by erudition and love of
God, leading their students through the dark night of mod-
ernism to an orthodoxy rejuvenated—not the neo-orthodoxy
recently popularized by the Swiss theologian Karl Barth, slippery equivocations on history with a slight demurral on the
resurrected body (not to mention the rumor of a mistress); but
an orthodoxy unreconstructed and stolid, born of Scottish and
Dutch sensibilities, proud and tough, like the work of J. Gre-
sham Machen of the Westminster school or of Berkower and
Bavink of the Freie Universiteit, built on the foundations of

truth, reason, and verification, fortified with a deliberate piety and common sense.

Families sent their daughters to Belhaven on the conviction that Mississippi's finishing schools were as good as Virginia's. They were certainly less pretentious. Gillespie might have misgivings about exposing his girls to the poetry of the pantheist Wordsworth or the bedrugged Coleridge—not to mention the New Criticism and the fashionable moral torpor inspired therefrom.[4] Still, he indulged the study of literature, arranged for readings of Mississippi authors and performances of traveling theater companies, and funded a literary magazine and a society of letters that encouraged creative writing.

At Belhaven, my mother was also introduced to contemporary poetry and novels under the tutelage of Sally Ransom. Sally's brother, John Crowe Ransom, was the reigning poet laureate of the Southern Agrarians at Vanderbilt, but known more popularly as one of the twelve contributors to *I'll Take My Stand*, a book that approximated the literati's version of Citizens' Council sentiment: "Let the negro sit beneath his own vine and fig tree," and so on. Sally Ransom taught my mother the simple elegance of cadence and meter and pushed her to take risks in her writing, to reach for a controlled but spontaneous effect. President Gillespie allowed intellectual innovation in the arts that he'd never grant to matters of faith and doctrine.

Myra Toler's essays were exemplary pieces of scholarship that moved gracefully from thesis to argument in a careful, comprehensive pacing, written with a formal eloquence. By the end of her freshman year, she could craft doctrine to the supreme satisfaction of her mentors. "God having created man upright, and he having sought out many inventions, and thus fallen into sin, our first inquiry must be into the remedy which God's love and mercy found for this fall," begins her introductory exposition on "The Covenant of Grace and Its Relation to Missions."

> This remedy, in its exhibition, was of course subsequent to the ruin; but when we consider it in its inception in the Divine mind, we must go back into the recesses of a past eternity. God ever foreknew all things; and all His works, unto the end, are according to His original, eternal plan. Conceiving of God's eternal decree then in parts (the only mode of conception of it competent to our finite minds) we must consider that part of His plan formed from eternity, which was implied in that other part of the same plan whereby He purposed to permit man's fall and ruin. This remedial part of God's decree is the thing which the more recent Calvinistic divines term the *Covenant of Grace*.

If one my students had turned in this paper, I would no doubt have had to fight off suspicions of plagiarism. But my mother regarded her studies as a form of worship, and for a budding Calvinist intellectual, the worship of the Holy God must be perfect and pure. "Every detail in every moment of the life of the race is God-determined," she wrote. "And it is through the divine government of these things, which is in short the leading onwards of the race to salvation that the great goal is at last attained."

Though she missed her high school friends and sometimes felt a little blue at the thought of those years now vanished like a dream, she seized on the academic life with all her might. In the cool of the morning, before the sunrise, she'd begin her days in prayer at her father's desk on the sleeping porch, and read until she left for classes. Often she would not return home until the library closed at ten o'clock, walking the two blocks beneath the soft glow of the streetlights, her mind alive with the writings of John Milton and Hermann Bavink, and Walter de la Mare, her favorite. She finished her freshman year with straight A's and the praise of her teachers. In the spring of 1954, she was named the junior marshal of the college.

While most of her Jackson friends had their eyes set on the debutante summer ahead, my mother politely explained that she'd rather spend time in prayerful consideration of God's will for her life, in the study of Scripture and sacred doctrine, in the company of her friends in the church youth group. She also realized that the debutante crowd was not her kind of her people, sparing herself full recognition of the fact that she would never feel completely at home among the local Brahmin.

Lillian Toler's response to her daughter's decision to decline the social whirl was a condescending shrug to anyone who presumed the advantage of invitation, so developed were her own self-constructions of aristocracy. Her Swedish father hailed from the purest Nordic stock, nephew of the famed naturalist Zellerstedt, and son of a sea captain. A pen-and-ink sketch of the family church in Ronnerby hung on the wall by her dresser. On the maternal side, a document from the Jamestown Society certifying the early trip over could be produced as evidence. Jackson's social elite was as dung compared with the noble Hubbard lineage, which flourished in Mississippi, despite Emancipation, on a two-thousand-acre plantation near Lumberton, homestead of her beloved great-uncle Billy. "'I'm not ashamed of the fact that I belonged to the Ku Klux Klan,'" Billy Hubbard said in a 1921 interview with the *Hattiesburg American*—"his eyes gleaming with a strange fire as the blood of his Saxon ancestry shot through his veins." Lillian's fabled forefathers had shed their blood for Southern sovereignty, turned back the heathen with a steady gun, the burning cross, and a rapier wit (forgetting for a minute the Swedish newcomers). "'We had to run out the carpetbaggers and the scalawags to restore white supremacy, and we did it,'" Uncle Billy said. "'Somber cedars and spectral glints of tombstones in the middle of the night held no fears for our determined hand.'"

Kenneth, my mother's father, had as little interest in the world of bridge parties and coming-out balls ("De-Butts" he said) as in attending the First Presbyterian Church ("the unofficial chapel of the Citizens' Council"). He despised Mississippi good ole' boys, their thin veneer of amiability, their smirky quips, the seething meanness below. He preferred a booth at the Elite Café over a church pew and Sunday devotionals with self-righteous boors; smoky conversations with his newspaper friends Bill Minor, who wrote the "Eyes on Mississippi" column for the *New Orleans Times–Picayune*, and John Herbers, the *New York Times* Mississippi correspondent. Kenneth's pleasures were simple and straight: shoptalk with his colleagues, bourbon whiskey, ballroom dancing at the Buena Vista Hotel, the L.S.U. Fighting Tigers (with whom he had played single-wing flanker for one brief but glorious season), and the annual Toler-Charchere "Lou Wee's" fest in Opelousas. This was all the society he needed. Kenneth liked being an outsider—it gave him the advantage of seeing things differently—and wasn't about to give up his Crowley, Louisiana, patois for the cackly drawl of the Hinds County blue blood.

Anyway, he loved his four daughters fiercely, whatever they decided to do about society or God, and he told them that and more: They were more precious than angels. He didn't need a goddamned summer cotillion as further proof.

Society seemed even less attractive to Myra after she met Bob Marsh at a Youth for Christ meeting at the downtown Heidelberg Hotel. Bob had graduated from Baylor in May with a B.A. in history and was working in Jackson for the summer before moving to New Orleans to begin seminary in the fall. His yellow hydromatic Dodge with a convertible top became a regular sight on Fairview Street. Friday nights he accompanied her to youth crusades and afterward to the Seallily Drive-In for root beer floats. With the sounds of the summer night in the fields beyond the parking lot, the two would talk of their lives so far, about their friends and fun times shared—and increasingly of the great goodness that had brought them together. At summer's end at a Bible camp in Biloxi, he declared his love for her, beside the gulf waters on a moonlit night.

When he began studies in September of 1953 at the Baptist Theological Seminary in New Orleans, he wrote her daily from his dorm on Gentilly Boulevard.

How I have longed and missed you so terribly much today. Myra, it can't be too soon for me to marry. I want you more and more every day. How can anyone love as I love you. Myra, I am yours forever and completely. You have me always.

There is so much on my heart tonight. I would give anything to be with you and talk to you. Oh, dear, I can't stand being away from you.

Sweetheart, there seem so many little problems in the way, but don't you believe the Lord will work them out? I believe He is leading in our marriage and although it looks difficult now, I believe He will supply all our needs somehow.

I really am hopeless and sometimes I feel so bad about it. Myra, I do hope you will never be disappointed or regret it. I wish I could give you the finer things, but I know I'll never be a "big shot" or have much income. God only knows the future, I don't, but I am so thankful for you, my sweetheart. It is too good to really imagine that you are mine. Myra, I love you so deeply, so very much.

By the middle of the fall, she was writing him daily.

Everything in my life is in you. I love you so much. I am so happy with you and so proud that you are mine, I want you Bob more than anything in the world. I want to marry you and have you for always.

Won't it be wonderful having each other—to be together for a life— living for Jesus—and facing the happy times and the hard times together. I love you and am yours forever.

My love for you grows deeper—it is so strong that it makes me ache. Bob, I love you with all my heart and life. I am yours for eternity.

Some of her letters would be sent to the seminary, others to backwater outposts where he preached revival crusades, in Mississippi towns like Hernando and Magnolia and Hot Coffee. He was not the intellectual she may have once thought she wanted. He didn't subscribe to the minutiae of Reformed dogma as she did—he didn't even understand them, couldn't care less. But he gave himself to his preaching with a passion she seldom encountered in her Calvinist up-bringing. And that more than compensated for his academic mediocrity and his constitutional impatience with the every-day.

Their letters acknowledged life's uncertainties: hers a de-sire for a pure heart, for the courage "to lean not to her own understanding," to be his helpmate; his the fears and uncer-tainties of life, the difficulty of standing confidently before God. She accepted his proposal in marriage, although she had only completed her first year at Belhaven and would soon give up hopes of finishing her degree. The two were married in the summer of 1954, at the First Presbyterian Church of Jackson, and according to the *Clarion-Ledger* article, "against a back-ground arrangement of magnolia foliage and blush pink blos-soms, towering white candles in white-turned wood candelabras lining the choir rail, while single white tapers glowed on either side of the prie dieu."

That summer the tiny Steen's Creek Baptist Church in the town of Florence, Mississippi, offered my father a job and the newlyweds moved into the parsonage next door. On Sundays and Wednesdays, before a sleepy congregation of born-and-raised Christian folks, he pleaded and cajoled and wrung his hands for their salvation. On Mondays, Tuesdays, Thursdays, and Fridays, he worked toward his bachelor of divinity at the seminary, sometimes driving six hours down and back the same day. Between classes, or sometimes after cutting classes, he took to the streets of the French Quarter and confronted the winos in Pirate's Alley. He preached in Jackson Square and blitzed the honky-tonks and strip joints on Bourbon Street, arming his body with the breastplate of righteousness—his red-leather King James Bible and a tight-fitting polo shirt—and pulling the plug on the jukebox. He defied the rage of the heathens with the plain fact that they might run but they couldn't hide, the miracle of Jesus suffering for bums like these. He hollered and howled until they saw themselves for what they were, sinners bound for hell, "filled with all unrighteousness, fornication, wickedness, and deceit." They'd not be spared God's righteous anger, or his for that matter.

My father craved preaching like a drowning man craved air. All he wanted was to preach. He accepted invitations at country churches and tent revivals. He preached in cinderblock school buildings and at river meetings; in little league ballparks and on the back of flatbed trucks. "The Lord gave us a good service tonight. We are also having morning services," he wrote after a tent meeting in Picayune. "We saw several young people come to the Lord. But it is such a heartache; there is so much indifference to spiritual things. Pray! Pray! Pray much for God to send down upon us a real revival!"

His stuttering would sometimes flicker back to life in everyday comings and goings, in a seminary presentation, or at a cookout in the backyard of one of Myra's old friends from Central High, but when he gave himself to the business of saving lost souls, he felt pulled out of ordinary time into a world alive with power and passion, and his tongue flashed freely like living fire.

7

Church Boy

On Sunday mornings the streets of Laurel were filled with churchgoers. In the historic neighborhood near the downtown churches, men and women and children walked along the brick sidewalks, holding hands in the fine air or sharing parasols in the rain or beneath a hot sun; from the surrounding neighborhoods, late-model automobiles arrived in the parking lots carrying more families dressed to the nines. Sunday School began at 9:30 a.m., followed by the main worship service at 11:00 a.m., but I was always there at least a half hour early, since my mother helped the members of the Women's

Missionary Union set up the coffee and iced-tea table in the
fellowship hall. Our early arrival meant an early wake-up,
along with the requirement to dress up, which together made
Sunday mornings my least favorite time of the week. I knew I
should have felt different, since it was after all the "day of the
Lord," set aside by law and custom, to reckon with our spiritual welfare. But the fact was, I dreaded Sundays above all
other days.

For me, "looking my best for God" involved a white cotton
shirt, starched stiff as drywall, and a pair of maroon double-
knit trousers. And it involved distressing side effects. Cotton
stretches; polyester contracts. This grim fact I discovered
thanks to the sudden yank of wedges and crinkles, tickling up
into every crevice from the time I stooped into the Impala for
the ride to church. Much effort was spent before Sunday
School in the white-marble bathroom in the church foyer,
tucking cotton shirts into tight pants, rearranging underwear
and body parts, and smoothing over awkward bulges. Yet by
the end of the first verse of "Rise and Shine and Give God the
Glory," which we sang in the general assembly before splitting
up into "boys-only" and "girls-only" sections, everything had
once again come undone. The urge to shake myself free of
torment, ferociously satisfied any other time of the week, had
to be suppressed now by a nearly heroic act of the will.
Droplets of sweat appeared on my scalp, fanned out across my
forehead. I grew jittery and cross, and sometimes broke into
thunderous vibrato (which earned me the evil eye of the Sunday School director but the heartfelt appreciation of the other

boys). Most of the time, however, I accepted my fate and performed like a church boy.

The Bible study was solemn as a wake. First, we read the
weekly selections, one boy for each verse, moving clockwise
around the table. Our teacher, Mr. Phillips, didn't consider it
funny in the least if one of us botched the names of Abimelech
and Zerubbabel (or the ever hilarious Titas), or places like
Ezion-gaber or Assos. We were usually forced to try every
pronunciation imaginable before getting bailed out. We were
then asked questions on the reading, and once again moved
clockwise around the table, one boy for each question until
the list was finished. The Sunday School board's complete lack
of metaphysical curiosity expedited matters considerably. If
the passage read, "And Jesus being full of the Holy Ghost returned from Jordan, and was led by the Spirit into the wilderness, being forty days tempted of the devil," we were likely to
be quizzed on matters of geography and duration. A good answer was "from Jordan," "forty days," and the like. Mr. Phillips
considered further inquiries on our part impious ("Why does
everything take forty days?" "You're saying she was seven hundred years old when she got pregnant?") and were not to be
tolerated.

Finally, Mr. Phillips opened his spiral-bound "Disciple's
Guide" and read the lesson of the day. Other teachers would
later take stabs at amplification or comic relief. Not Phillips.
He read the lesson straight out of the guidebook, word for
word, and in a monotone that weighed upon us like an August
sun. Our eyelids grew heavy. Our breathing slowed to Zen-
like rhythms. We tried our best to pay attention, if only to sal-

vage some presence of mind for the concluding discussion. But by the time he had finished the last sentence of the lesson, we had collectively reached some cognitive state beyond hypnosis and stupefaction. After a few failed attempts to share a spiritual insight or word of edification—"I heard Bubba Jones found Jesus at the crusade last night"—we were dispatched to the eleven o'clock worship service and released from our misery.

Following another round of tucking and untucking in the white-marble bathroom, I began the ascent to the last row of the balcony. These hinterlands of the sanctuary served as the gathering spot of choice for the young people, except when an older student made a "profession of faith in Christ," walking the aisle at the sermon's end as a public expression of his salvation. He would then take up residence in the front rows nearest the pulpit, at least for the next few weeks prior to his baptism, after which he would eventually drift back up to the balcony. From our perch, we could whisper, throw spitballs, or play hangman without distraction. Sports scorecards, clipped out of the morning newspaper and tucked into the pages of the *Baptist Hymnal*, could be studied by groups of twos and threes. We might even appear prayerful to someone sitting in another part of the sanctuary and receive compliments after church on our behavior.

But after the offering was collected and the crescendos of the special music earned a few hoarse "Amens," all our diversions were put away. The time of the sermon had arrived. It was not the fear of our parents that prompted us to open our Bibles and sit straight as soldiers—or of head usher Ralph Simmons patrolling the balcony with a watchdog eye and a nerve-pinching grip. It was the certainty that the Almighty himself was about to speak. My father was his chosen instrument, and we were the chaff of his threshing. The sermon was our body and blood, the verbal satisfaction of our old-time religion, sacramental partner of our midweek feasts of chicken and trimmings, but it must satisfy by admonishing, convicting, and agitating.

My father was well prepared for the task. He roamed the breadth of the stage like a pacing lion. We followed his movements and the trail of his words as though our lives hung in the balance—arms raised in a field of fire, *God's mercy upon us*, arms now extended in Golgotha's horror, *atonement for humanity's wickedness*, arms embracing a dying child, tears in his eyes and in ours, *the infinite sorrow of innocence slain*. We listened as the world's pagan hopes sank into death's silences. The pulpit itself became nothing but a prop for his ice water.

He asked, What would it profit us if we gained fame and fortune but could not save our souls? Think of the sacrifice of God's only son, his sunset cry redirecting creation toward its high calling. Such kindness could not be shunned without a price. What would it profit us on that last day, when Jesus returns in the sky for his children, if we were proud and mighty in our own eyes but corrupt in the eyes of God?

And I wondered, What if I were riding my bicycle one afternoon and while I crossed Old Bay Springs Road to the sidewalk as I have done a thousand times before, I forgot *this time* to check both ways for oncoming traffic? What if instead I kept riding, two feet, three feet, four feet into the road, and then a car, driven by a teenager with whiskey on his breath, or a housewife smoking a thin cigarette, or a doctor hurrying to an afternoon dalliance, all thinking the boy on the bicycle would hug the shoulder of the road long enough for the car to pass, crushed me into the black asphalt? Would I be ready to meet Jesus? Would my name be found in the Book of Life? Sure, I never miss church. Sure, I'm from a godly family. I'm polite to my elders. Well-mannered and obedient. But am I ready? My father wanted to know. His arms pounded the pulpit, pounded the air, beseeched God on our behalf. *Open their eyes, stir their consciences, torment them until they call your name.*

What if I were sitting in the school auditorium on a Friday morning, watching the weekly civics movie, and one minute my classmates and I are luxuriating in mindless contentment, sunny images of migrant workers and public buildings floating by in dreamlike succession, and the next minute all is a great chaos, a sudden vanishing of friends and enemies, the Rapture? And yet what if *I* remained in my chair until the film comes to an end—savagely spit from the projector like hypocrites from the mouth of God? *I've been left behind.* My family's house at 8 Highland Woods would still be standing. Our two cars would still be parked in the driveway, an olive-green Impala and the red Opal Cadet (where I could still find a box of my father's Ayds diet chocolates melting between the bucket seats). I could throw open the screen door of the porch, but mother would not be standing by the window with a cup of coffee in her hand, because she has been taken up to meet Jesus in the sky with millions of living and millions more

sleeping, now-awakening souls. Was I ready for this day, a day
we shall all someday face, at an hour no man knows?

The question gripped me the first time I heard it, and
every time thereafter. Could anything be sadder than a silence
without end or measure? "Mom?" "Dad?" "Spot?"

My father wiped his brow, took a sip of ice water, turned
back to the listening congregation, and said, Yes, in fact,
something could.

I do not like the idea of Hell. But my feelings concerning a fact
will not alter a fact. I do not like disease, but disease is a fact.
And Hell is a fact—of that I must remind you.

Hell is an eternal place of everlasting separation from God.
Hell is an eternal place of everlasting anguish. In Hell, a person
goes on existing in a state that can be described only in terms of
absolute ruin, anguish, torment. But the torment of Hell is ac-
centuated by the punishment of memory and conscience. Once
you have said no to Christ for the last time, you sin against His
love for the last time, once the great gates of death close behind
you and you awaken in eternity to the awesome realization that
you are in Hell, you will hear resounding across the corridors of
endless time "Forever," "Forever," "Forever."

My father stood motionless before us, his two arms pointing downward in petition, his face a study in agony.

If I could find in the Bible some faint glimpse to state that
after you had been in Hell 100,000 years that there would be
hope, I would give it to you. But I can't. For how long will there
be the awful fact of Hell? As long as there is the blessed fact of

Heaven. How long will a lost soul remember the sin of rejection, suffer the agony of a condemning conscience, endure the path of separation from God? As long as God lives upon the throne of the universe. This the horror of Hell.

Here is a young man playing it loose in sexual immorality, forgetting that the fire cannot be taken to the bosom without hurt being the end result; a young man treating people as things rather than as creatures of human dignity; and we say to this fellow who denies decency and lives on the level of lust—don't you realize that whatsoever a man sows, he is going to reap?

A young lady pandering away her purity upon the altar of popularity and pleasure, selling her virtue for thrills which pass away, turning over respect for a perverted romance, desiring sophistication more than spirituality, don't you realize that the wages of sin is death?—but she doesn't care, she's having a ball.

My father placed his fist beneath his chin now in mock concentration.

Some self-styled ecclesiastical scholars atop their academic ivory towers have led us down dark alleys of offbeat theology and have said to us, Scoff at this old-fashioned idea of Hell, a medieval concept of outdated theology; scoff at this doctrine of Hell, it is just a trick of the evangelist to scare the children and frighten the simple-minded.

Hah, hah, we hear from colleges that are erupting with the conflagration of immorality. Hah, hah, we hear from some pulpits where the churches are glorified icebergs floating on the nebulous sea of liberalism. Hah, hah, we hear from some Virginia Woolf sophisticate whose god is pleasure and whose life is filled with anxiety and confusion.

My father squared off and grimaced, shaking his head in disbelief. He slowly raised his arms in supplication.

If you have not heard a word I have said, listen to me now. I will tell you of the heartbreaking lesson of fatal carelessness.

A man looked me in the eyes one day and said, "Preacher, I just cannot make up my mind about giving my life to Christ. I don't know what to do," Time settled it for him. A few days later he was in his coffin. Was he in Hell? Yes, if he failed to trust Christ and give his life to the Lord.

Time, like water spilled on the ground, cannot be gathered up again. The clock that strikes the midnight hour tonight will never strike on the same day again. Time, once it has been recorded, can never be recalled. It works like this: The little child says, "There is plenty of time, I am young yet." See the same child later in his tender teens. He is busy with school, dates, sports, living it up. There is plenty of time. "I just want to have fun," he says. There he is in his tempestuous twenties, marriage, a whirl of social events, the excitement of a career begun, plenty of time. See the man in his tired thirties, cares lining his face, too busy now for religion, plenty of time. There he is in his feverish forties, hair turning gray, troubles mounting, but plenty of time. See him in his frantic fifties, plenty of time. In his sinking sixties, plenty of time. See that man in his solemn seventies, trembling and tottering on the brink of the grave. There is still time! There is still time! But suddenly a slip of the glass, crash, and then out of the blackness of eternal despair rushes his soul to meet God, unprepared because of fatal carelessness.

When my father concluded the sermon, or sometimes even before the final words had been spoken (if the organist detected in his voice the penultimate lilt toward the salvation summons), the invitational hymn began to play. In one of my earliest memories, I'm sitting on the floor of my bedroom in our house in Mobile, where I lived until my fourth birthday. My poplin suit has been dispensed with; several piles of clothing bear the evidence of a morning at church. I am holding a tin Confederate soldier, singing the words of this hymn:

> *All to Jesus I surrender, all to him I freely give;*
> *I will ever love and trust him, in his presence daily live.*
> *I surrender all, I surrender all;*
> *All to Thee, my blessed Savior, I surrender all.*

No matter that I had confused the Lost Cause and the Divine Call, not an unusual mistake for a Southern boy like me: The fact was there could be no turning back.

What did I learn in all those Sunday mornings in the cavernous, iconless sanctuaries of my childhood? I learned that every nod toward meaning counts, big time. I learned that I could never let down my guard in the few and fleeting days of our mortal life.

The literary critic James Wood, who grew up in a conservative Christian family in northern England, once said that whether or not the "child of evangelicalism" continues to believe in God as an adult, he "inherits nevertheless a suspicion of indifference."[1] "Mild-mannered religion," in my father's sneering words, could never be an option, nor could mild-mannered unbelief. Even if the child buries evangelical belief, says Wood, "he has not buried the evangelical choice, which seems to him the only important dilemma." God or nothing, purity or ruin. Beliefs about doctrine may alter over time, endure the blows of revision and demythologization, *aufheben* into forms less literal, archaic, neurotic. Beliefs may disappear altogether—"a pointlessness posing as a purpose," in Wood's estimation. Yet, the passion never ends: The child "is always evangelical."

On a moonlit night, I burned Ouija boards to defy the powers of darkness.

I smashed my "Chipmunks Sing the Beatles" album against a pine tree when John Lennon made his famous boast about being more popular than Jesus.

I offered up my body as a living sacrifice because I knew the ruin of my "old man."

I felt the Spirit's fire—boy, did I ever—but . . . I couldn't let it loose.

My problem was never with the simple story "love one another, as I have loved you"—though I could have used more of the simple story. The way of unbelief has always seemed too easy to me, a retreat of the imagination posing as a purpose. My problem was I just really needed some breathing room.

White evangelicals like my family lived their lives inside a paradox: Our desire for God was still desire, the same kind that aches until it's filled, overwhelms its intended object—personal relationship with Jesus—and then licks wildly for contact like flames in a brushfire. Maybe if I'd been Catholic, the whole thing would have felt different. You ascend the scale of erotic love and in the end you find God. Misfires and screwups, the dumbest deeds imaginable, are all parts of the

journey, as long as the heart is true and you keep your sins forgiven. I've known plenty of guilty Catholics, but I've never
known one who would let guilt get in the way of a good time.
We preferred our *theos* straight up, untainted by *eros* and the
body's contrary needs, even though erotic energies consumed
us at every youth retreat and crusade. And so we turned freedom into bondage, risk into sameness, the world wide-open
into craft and gimmick. Never mind we worshiped a Jew who
broke all the rules, who showed us the grace in the unclean
and the hypocrisy of the pure, the Lord of beggars and
whores, enemy of the righteous. No, maybe our real problem
was not too much Jesus, but too little.

8

Birds of a Feather

The last autumn we lived in Alabama, in 1966, my family drove to Jackson for Thanksgiving. I remember the towns of Evergreen, Grove Hill, Meridian, and Forest, peaceful under the warm autumn sun. From the backseat of the car, I traced the rise and fall of electric lines with my finger, and, after a while, I fell asleep to the sounds of the lonesome highway. I woke up as our green Impala came to a stop at the Tolers' house on Fairview.

Inside, Grandma Lilly, as we called my mother's mother, guarded over the kitchen, while her four daughters chopped, cut, and sliced on demand. Everyone else knew to keep their distance. If you dared sneak in for a prelunch snack, you'd better be ready to pay the price. It was as if Lilly had sprung eyes in the back of her head and could swing a wooden spatula at a grandchild with one hand and continue stuffing turkey with the other. She'd grab a rolling pin or a skillet if you were hard of hearing. It didn't matter that lunch was hours away. If you tried telling her you were hungry now, she'd say good. That was how you were supposed to feel on Thanksgiving day. Now get out of the kitchen and leave me in peace.

My father never tested Lilly the way the grandchildren and other relatives did. His habit was to leave the house and take refuge at Primo's, the only diner in town open on Thanksgiving Day. Just going to look for a newspaper, he'd say. But I knew better, having gone along a few times myself and been sworn to secrecy. He'd stay at Primo's at least an hour, drinking coffee at the lunch counter, eating a bowl of grits with jelly and butter, maybe a fried egg on top.

My father was the one exception to Lilly's belief that no male member of her family was up to any good. Whatever he did was fine by her; she wasn't criticizing. The daughters suspected she had a crush on her son-in-law. She told everyone he looked like Paul Newman. A preacher Paul Newman at that, better than the real thing. Lilly would even get herself rebaptized by him—immersed in water in the Baptist fashion—though she never doubted the Presbyterian sprinkling of infants.

It was a different story with me though. If I'd gone along, she'd be waiting at the front door when I got back as if she'd been there the whole time. She'd sniff around my mouth like a bloodhound, inspect my clothing, my breath, the expression on my face. If she spied a cookie crumb on my collar or caught a whiff of vanilla, she'd slap her bony hand against my chest and holler, "Dawgonnit, Myra! Charles has gone and lost his appetite. Dawgonnit!" She'd hit me again with her hand and walk off in disgust.

My grandfather, Kenneth Toler, also made himself scarce until lunch, hiding out in his chair on the sleeping porch, working the *New York Times* crossword puzzle, dozing with a cigar curled between his fingers. He got up when it was time to carve the turkey and offer his annual blessing. A simple "Peace!" followed by a pontifical wave of the hand. Eat, for heaven's sake

And we ate. Turkey and oyster casserole, cornbread stuffing with sweet onions, asparagus hollandaise, candied yams, English peas (from the obligatory LeSeur can, the only acceptable prepared food), rice and gravy, corn muffins, and cranberry sauce. Desserts waited on the sideboard: pecan and pumpkin pies, a mountain of ambrosia. Charlotte russe chilled in the fridge.

Our table was full. The youngest daughter, my aunt Binky, was home from Erskine College. Aunt Emily, the third daughter, and her husband, Wilson, the theologian, had come up from New Orleans with their two children. The next to oldest daughter, Cecile, and her family were coming later for dessert, although no one expected them to be on time. Cecile, the next to oldest child, had married a wealthy planter from the Louisiana Delta, who shortly after the wedding renounced his birthright for a simple life and forbade his wife to wear jewelry, makeup, or dresses above midcalf. Cecile had given birth to a child every year since their marriage in 1962, and the brood made travel difficult. But even if the five young ones were packed in good time, her husband Phinn could not make the two-hour drive to Jackson without stopping along the way to witness for the Lord. Phinn believed in angels, the kind described in the *Epistle to the Hebrews*, so service station attendants, hoboes, waitresses in diners, and highway drifters became tests of faith, a potential rubbing shoulders with "angels unawares."

One sweltering summer day, I was riding in the Hogues' un-air-conditioned station wagon when Phinn pulled to the shoulder of the road to evangelize a hitchhiker. While Phinn and his Test of Faith, beneath a lunchtime sun, huddled over the pages of a pocket-sized New Testament, I remained in the car with the children, slowly turning the color of cooked beets. When Phinn finished his work, he wished the man godspeed and abandoned him in the furnace of the roadside.

Uncle Hilliard, Lilly's only brother, his wife Vema, and their only child Flora-Jane were down from Kosciusko. Uncle Hilliard, a short wiry man resembling Fred Astaire, chain-smoked Tareytons and helped found the Citizens' Council in his hometown. When the subject of race came up, and it almost always did in his company, he eyes would narrow and his voice would quiver. You'd never know that two decades earlier he had lived the bohemian life as an artist in New Orleans. He rented a one-bedroom apartment on Toulouse Street and painted watercolors of Delta shanties, of Negro men with gunpowder hair and watery eyes, of black boys fishing from a wooden bridge. He claimed a space along Jackson Square and sold his art to tourists. By the end of the fall, when the weather had grown raw and gray, Hilliard ran out of money. So he quit New Orleans, with regrets of the artist's life abandoned but with a Depression child's sober acquiescence, and took a job as an industrial designer in Kosciusko, spending his days in front of a metal desk making sketches of shipping containers and luggage trunks. Somewhere along the way he got angry and—like most angry whites in those days—decided that the South's racial turmoil was as good an explanation as any for the harsh blows of life come his way.

We'd gotten through the turkey and oysters. I was still eating a drumstick, but that didn't stop Lilly from yanking my plate out from under me to take back to the kitchen. "You've been eating long enough," she said. "And I'm tired of hearing you smack your food. Sounds like rats in the attic."

My grandfather Kenneth was stirring a fist of rice into his milk glass, adding a spoonful of sugar to sweeten the mixture. The daughters were serving dessert and coffee.

Uncle Hilliard was smoking again now in the pause between eating. He leaned back in his chair and tilted his head slightly upward the way he did before commencing to speak. I didn't get much of what he was talking about at the time, being barely ten years old. But it didn't even take a ten-year-old to figure out that Hilliard was mightily concerned about "the Negro problem." Later on I managed to stitch together more.

"I read your piece yesterday evening," he said to my grandfather. "You can't be too hard on those birds is how I see it."

"Stokely's just a loudmouth," Kenneth said with a smile. "He's a nuisance. You've got that right. But I hear he wouldn't hurt a fly."

My grandfather had written a story about Stokely Carmichael's latest visit to Jackson, during which the activist performed his successful role as screaming militant before getting himself arrested and jailed again.

But before my grandfater could finish, Hilliard was waving his hands in protest, and saying excitedly, "That is just pure hog-dukey. And you know I love you, don't you. I really do. But that is just pure hog-dukey."

"Hilliard!" his wife said into her shoulder. Flora-Jane and I giggled.

"That boy's been flying all over kingdom come talking about the communist overthrow of America. Talking about how great a man Castro is. How Russians are better than Americans. You're just not seeing this thing straight."

Lilly let out a sympathetic moan followed by a clearing of the throat. "I'll agree with you about that, my brother Hilliard," it seemed to suggest, "but put a lid on it now." The daughters were looking into their cups.

Uncle Fortner, the theologian, cleared his throat and said, "Perception depends on the way images are manipulated by the controlling elites," adjusting his black-rimmed glasses as he spoke. Wilson had read theology at Oxford and recently written a series of articles for a popular religious journal in which he likened "the monster of prejudice" to buffoonery, peppering his reflections on the Cross with anecdotes from *Catcher in the Rye* and *Breakfast at Tiffany's*. Most of the family thought he had brought some liberal ideas back from England—but I knew for a fact that he kept a loaded pistol in the side pocket of his Volkswagen Bug. Wilson rarely spoke up in conversation, preferring to finish his meal and get back to the sleeping porch where a mystery novel awaited. But today was different. He had a point to make. "You might be interested to know that McLuhan thinks—"

"How's the situation in Alabama?," Hilliard asked my father, cutting Wilson off in midsentence. He wasn't interested in the least. And Hilliard did not mean the spiritual welfare of our congregation. He wanted to know what we were doing to keep our Negroes in line.

My father hated talking politics, especially when he was eating. He hated talking about anything controversial when he was eating, politics or religion. Zealots like Hilliard never seemed to have the good sense to know when to keep their mouths shut, he thought, and it was this, really, that made them most irritating.

"Oh, we're doing just fine," he said, trying to be as vague and noncommittal as possible in an effort to avoid Hilliard's bait. "We've got some good folk in the state, and I think we'll be fine."

"Damn right you got some good folk," Hilliard said.

"Lawd have mercy, Hilliard, hush your mouth!" said Lilly, throwing her napkin his way. She got up from her chair and walked into the kitchen.

"Got some solid Councilors over there. Got some Klan, too. Damn right you'll be fine."

"We're real blessed with good church leadership," my father smiled. He turned his head slightly toward the front window as if anticipating a distant sound.

My father's comment perked me up. I had been eating a large piece of pecan pie with sugar-cream poured on top, but I knew something about this. "We really do have good leadership in Andalusia, Uncle Hilliard. You won't believe what they gave us last month for our fifth anniversary. A color television! Did you know that Maxwell Smart's car is red? I didn't know that. And so is Opie's hair. It's amazing what you can see watching a color TV."

Hilliard was on his second black coffee.

"I didn't know that, son. That's real interesting," Hilliard said to me with a smile.

"But, now, Bob, it doesn't matter to me what kind of church leadership you've got," he'd turned back to my father. "The important thing is to keep the nigras from going wild."

"The Holy Spirit is doing something special at First Baptist," my father added.

"Doesn't matter to me what the Holy Spirit's doing. I hate to say this. You know I love you and Myra, don't you?"

But my mother had just left the room, too, along with her sisters, to join Lilly in the kitchen. I heard them washing dishes and laughing. Outside the afternoon sunlight cut through the thin leaves of the crepe mertle tree. The air was warm and balmy.

"You might be right about Stokely." Kenneth was talking now. "He may be a Red. Hell, he may be a lunatic. But what I do know is that most Negroes just want a fair deal. I can't see why that's got you and everybody else so upset."

My grandfather was known as a man who rarely offered his opinion. He liked the facts, plain and simple, even though facts alone could get you into heaps of trouble in Mississippi. Kenneth Toler worked for *The Memphis Commercial Appeal* covering Mississippi politics, and was considered outside the South as one of the region's few trustworthy reporters. From the press room of the state Capitol, where he worked when the legislature was in session, or from his office in the King Edward Hotel, Kenneth Toler dared to tell Jim Crow's dirty secrets. "A startling revelation," he wrote in a 1957 column, "with no bearing on the school count, is the disparity in the per capita expenditures between the races. It is so much out of line in proportion to the number of educable in each race to give cause for alarm." White children received an average expenditure in excess of $200, he explained, while the educational support for Negroes remained at a "pitiful low" of $25. "Little wonder Mississippi Negroes are demanding, rather than asking, for a semblance of equality."

A decade earlier, in 1946, he'd exposed the demagogic Theodore G. Bilbo as a know-nothing and a bully. Theodore Bilbo, the former Mississippi governor seeking reelection to the U.S. Senate, had told white voters that the best way to solve the racial problem was to put every single American Negro on a boat back to Africa. Throughout his political life, Bilbo fought against Negro rights, antilynching laws, the repeal of the poll tax, or any other legislation directly or indirectly

improving the lot of black Southerners. During his 1946 campaign for the U.S. Senate—the first statewide contest in Mississippi since the U.S. Supreme Court had outlawed all-white
primaries two years earlier—Bilbo publicly threatened would-
be Negro voters: "If you let a handful go to the polls in July,
there will be two handfuls in 1947, and from there on it will
grow into a mighty surge."[1] With his hand shaking the air, and
his eyes bulging like an insect's, he had told white Mississippians that they were "sleeping on a volcano." In Bilbo's estimation, there was only one sure way to keep the racial fires from
burning. "You do it the night before the election. I don't have
to tell you any more than that. Red-blooded men know what I
mean."[2]

Kenneth refused to let Bilbo's "reign of terror" and thinly
veiled threats of lynching go unreported. He penned a series
of articles on the senator's election-eve remarks and the re-
pressive actions stemming therefrom, casting his support behind the Mississippi Negroes filing complaints with the U.S.
Senate Committee to Investigate Campaign Expenditures. "29
Witnesses Testify as Bilbo Trial Opens: Stories of Whipping,
Refusal of Right to Register Told by Many Negroes," read my
grandfather's front-page story on December 2, 1946. "State
election laws and a 'white supremacy at the ballot box' sentiment existent in Mississippi since Civil War days, bore the
brunt for failure of Negro participation in last summer's Democratic primary." Kenneth's articles became like a theater of
black voices, twenty-nine characters taking the stage in a
chilling drama of harassment and intimidation.

The Rev. William Albert Bender, Negro faculty member of Tougaloo College in Madison County, north of Jackson, and president of the Jackson NAACP Chapter, said he encountered no difficulty in registering, but when he went to the polls to vote a deputy sheriff "with a pistol in his pocket" dared him to enter the polling place and vote. He said he left and did not vote. Earlier, three men outside the polling place told him they were not permitting Negroes to vote because "This is a white man's Democratic party."

Edison Johnson, Negro college student of Jackson, testified he was afraid to vote because of Senator Bilbo's speeches and the burning of Ku Klux Klan crosses in this vicinity.

Willie D. Brown, barber of Greenville, said he was not successful in registering and that the Circuit clerk, a Mr. Cocks, he said, told him even if he answered questions about the Constitution as provided in determining qualifications of a voter, "it didn't matter, for no matter what he answered it would not be satisfactory to him (the Circuit clerk)."

Leon Dowdy, Greenville World War II veteran, said he tried five times to register without success and was told by the Circuit clerk that the "people put him in office and he wasn't going to stick his neck out by permitting Negroes to register."

John Hathorn, apprentice brick mason of Louisville [Mississippi] and veteran, said he was permitted to register, but did not vote because the Circuit clerk said if he did "there might be some disturbance." He said Senator Bilbo had made speeches against Negroes voting and advised him not to show up "as anything could happen."

Kenneth created a rare space in which Mississippi Negroes were able to tell their stories, an uncommon act of courage for a Southern newspaperman.

Lilly and her daughters had returned to the dining room. The ambrosia had been moved to the center of the table from the sideboard, and my mother was spooning the fruit and co- conut into smaller bowls and passing them around. I took an- other piece of pie instead.

My father was pouring cream into his coffee, fighting back a yawn.

"You're going to lose this battle, Hilliard," my grandfather continued. "And I hate to say *that*. In fact, you've already lost it. Our way of life was built on a faulty premise. We could call ourselves Christian and treat an entire race of men like ani- mals. One part of that equation had to collapse sooner or later. It's kind of funny, though, that both sides collapsed at the same time. The animals are speaking—and at times with real eloquence, you've got to admit—while the Christians are behaving like beasts."

Hilliard was sucking in cigarette smoke in short, rapid lungfuls.

"I don't understand a word you're saying," he said softly, looking straight at Kenneth. "But it's not over, my friend. I don't know how you can say that."

My father excused himself. He had to put some fine points on the Sunday sermon, he said. But when he stepped into the hallway, I heard the jangle of his car keys coming out of his pants pocket and the front door open. He wouldn't be back for hours.

Over the years, I'd witness similar scenes with my father, a direct response to a question or comment preempted by some sudden agitation. I came to refer to these moments as his "departures," but whether they were really prompted by agitation or cowardice, I couldn't always say. Every red-blooded pastor knows the value of a departure, the way they put off the chattering widow, the bossy parishioner, and youth directors with agendas. But my father's departures usually suggested something more to me—a profound annoyance bordering on anger—as though he'd had quite enough of whatever it was you were saying and was not about to take another word. You might be brilliant, or you might be stupid, but he was out of there. And just too polite to tell you to shut up.

Hilliard, Vema, and Flora-Jane thanked Lilly for the meal. They exchanged kisses with the daughters and departed for Kosciusko. I went out into the front yard to wait for my cousins, who had still not arrived. No doubt, the five of them were sitting on the shoulder of Highway 40, their father thumbing through the *Gospel of Mark* with some lonely highwayman. Two weeks later, my grandfather died of a massive heart attack, the result of too many cheap cigars and more social upheaval than any fair-minded Cajun could be expected to bear.

9

Onward Christian Terrorists

Throughout the fall of 1967, our first fall in Laurel, the Klan appeared with increasing frequency on the front page of the *Leader-Call*. As payback for the bad press he'd been getting from his hometown daily, Sam Bowers ordered the newspaper offices bombed. A few years earlier, a Klan bombing would have inspired a small-town daily to rethink its reporting. But now, after three years of murder and mayhem in the surrounding streets and environs, the once timid editors were digging in their heels. They still showed a disproportionate interest in the goings-on of black militants in De-

troit, Milwaukee, Chicago, Cincinnati, and other urban bat-
tlefields up North—as well as the blotter of black violence in
New York City. They followed the misadventures of H. Rap
Brown with as much interest as the preparations of the Ole
Miss football team. At least once a week, you would find
reprints of Brown's jivey harangues at some northeastern university, during a confrontation with police in New York City
or in some insurrectionary banana republic where he'd gone
to discuss the "third world coalition of revolutionaries who
were anticapitalist, anti-imperialist, and antiracist." "If America don't come around," he'd say, "we going to burn it down,
brother. Wage guerrilla warfare on the honkie white man!"[1]
But by the end of 1967, even Brown's escapades receded
from center stage, having been replaced by the local news.
On October 9, 1967, jury selection began for the trials of
eighteen local men charged in the 1964 murders of civil
rights workers Mickey Schwerner, James Chaney, and Andrew Goodman.

The murder had taken place on Sunday, June 21, just hours
after Mickey Schwerner returned from a Summer Project
training session in Oxford, Ohio. Schwerner, a Congress of
Racial Equality (CORE) worker in Meridian, along with James
Chaney (a local plasterer and fellow CORE activist) and Andy
Goodman (a volunteer from New York on his first day in Mississippi), had ridden together in a white station wagon along
State Highway 21 northward into Neshoba County. The
three men visited the Mt. Zion Methodist Church in the hamlet of Longdale, where members told of a horrifying night of
beatings and tortures they'd received as a result of opening

their doors to voter registration meetings. Shortly after their visit, Schwerner, Chaney, and Goodman were arrested by Deputy Sheriff Cecil Price in Neshoba County and jailed in downtown Philadelphia. Then on the orders of Sheriff Lawrence Rainey, they were released around 10:30 that same night, but were stopped a half hour later by Deputy Price after a high-speed chase. Price turned the three civil rights workers over to the eight Klansmen who had been waiting in a warehouse for the signal to move into action. After midnight, Schwerner, Chaney, and Goodman were taken to Rock Cut Road south of town and murdered. Just before Alton Wayne Roberts fired point-blank on Schwerner, Schwerner said, "Sir, I know just how you feel." Roberts turned and shot Andy Goodman in the chest. According to informant Doyle Barnette, Klansman John Jordan appeared in an automobile just after the two men had been shot, exclaiming, "Save one for me!" Jordan then jumped out and shot James Chaney in the back. "You didn't leave me nothing but a nigger," Jordan said, "but at least I killed me a nigger."[2]

Harold Cox, the bigoted U.S. district court judge in Meridian, would once again preside over a courtroom full of twittering Klansmen. Cox had played softball with the Klan in the earlier trials for the 1964 killings. He had once referred in court to black voting registrants as "a bunch of niggers . . . acting like a bunch of chimpanzees."[3] During the summer of 1964, he publicly stated his contempt for "those people [who] went to a church and were pepped up by a leather-lung preacher and then gathered in the streets like a massive dark cloud and descended on the clerk [to vote]."[4]

In 1965, government attorneys had succeeded in winning indictments against nineteen conspirators in the Neshoba County murders from a federal grand jury in Jackson.[5] But Cox dismissed all the substantive parts of the felony indictments and ruled that the Klansmen could be charged only with misdemeanors. In March the following year, the Justice Department appealed the 1965 decision to the U.S. Supreme Court, which overruled Judge Cox's decision and reinstated the indictments.[6] Perhaps the Supreme Court's rebuff, together with a failed but dramatic impeachment campaign against him in both houses of the U.S. Congress, had mellowed Judge Cox a bit over the years—or at least forced him to recognize the seriousness of the charges. In any case, on October 9, 1967, he surprised reporters, lawyers, and prospective jurors by opening the hearings eager to get down to business. "The law says you can serve if you are competent," he told the panel. "And, if you are competent, I'm going to make you serve."

The next day, the all-white jury was selected: five men and seven women, from working-class backgrounds, whose names and home addresses were printed on the front page of the *Leader-Call*. Federal prosecutors, led by John Doar, the assistant attorney general in the Civil Rights Section of the U.S. Justice Department, planned to bring conspiracy charges against Sam Bowers and seventeen other men (charges against one member of the original nineteen conspirators had been dropped). The charge of conspiracy to violate civil rights was a federal indictment created under a Reconstruction-era law and necessary because all federal murder charges in the Neshoba case had been dismissed in December 1964.[7] (No state charges were ever filed.) Conspiracy meant proving that the Four-teenth Amendment had been violated, that the victims had been injured, oppressed, threatened, and intimidated in the free "exercise and enjoyment" of their civil rights. Govern-ment prosecutors were seeking the maximum: ten years in prison and five thousand dollars in fines. Sam Bowers didn't seem worried at all. "A Mississippi jury would never convict a white man for killing a nigger," he said.

The day the 1967 trial began my father gave a talk on Christian character at a lunch gathering of civic leaders at the Pinehurst Hotel. "We need a burning faith," he told the audi-ence of Lion's Club members. "We can't make a strong civiliza-tion by ignoring God; by ignoring all that is decent and treating our fellow men as animals. While we have business as usual, there are termites that would destroy the foundations." But the Neshoba murders and the trials were the furthest thing from his mind. Secular humanism, greed, the lack of Christ-centered priorities, the "socialist cancer spreading the globe"—these were the real pests eating away at our strong civilization. "In this day of material gain, we are in grave dan-ger of destroying our foundations of freedom."

Not that he was inattentive to pagan eruptions on the home front. He complained of the garish advertisements for the Original Drive-In, located in an overgrown field on the outskirts of town, where teenagers parked their cars, drank beer, and petted heavily. Every afternoon in the sports section you'd find the playbills for movies like *Deadlier than the Male*, *Viva Las Vegas*, and *Goldfinger* in lush, lurid detail. Some people

might call this stuff "mature," he said, that along with the pro-
liferation of violence in Hollywood movies. But he preferred
to think of it as "filth." "What is happening to our nation when
we allow our children to sit for two hours watching Hollywood display glorified adultery and mocking decency and
morality?" he asked in his weekly column in the church bulletin.
"Is it old-fashioned to cry out for righteousness? Is it old-fashioned to call a people back to decency and purity? I say the
answer is yes, it's just as old-fashioned as the principles of personal discipline that made this nation great, and if we don't get
a large dose of some old fashioned virtue, our nation is gone."

To make matters worse, the season's startling new fashion
trend, the miniskirt, arrived one afternoon in the form of a
twelve-inch promotional flier featuring a curvy Parisian model
in a printed chiffon dress baring long legs and neck, her private parts adorned with ostrich feathers and lace. You could
accessorize, too, we learned in the ad, with stockings the
color of hot rum, windowpane, and crêpe suzette, making the
hop and skip from lecture hall to disco breezy and cool.

"Set your sights on spiritual things," became my father's re-
frain. Moral disintegration at home or abroad, the solution remained the same. "Without Jesus Christ, the whole house
collapses."

On a trip one evening to a popular hamburger stand in Ellisville, a town southeast of Laurel that required us to drive
past the Sambo Amusement Company near Masonite, my father talked to my mother and me about the trials. He wanted
us to know that they were nothing but the last gasp of a by-
gone era. "And I say good riddance to that," he exclaimed, as

we sped by the ramshackle buildings of the Sambo Amusement Company surrounded by chain-link fence. Laurel was a different place now from the way it had been a few years earlier. The civil rights movement had run its course, and although he was no fan of militants and troublemakers, he had to admit we were all probably a little better off as a result. He had spoken his mind in his Selma sermon and taken considerable risks for a Southern Baptist preacher. He had told white Christians in the South they needed to do better by Negroes, and that was not a popular thing to say. "No, the Klan will soon be history too," he said. "The good white people in this town aren't having any more of their shenanigans. You don't have to worry about that."

The White Knights' defense team, headed by Laurel Weir, was made up of "the entire practicing legal community of Neshoba County" (as one journalist noted). No fewer than fifty-seven witnesses were called in a seven-hour session to vouch for the character of the eighteen Klansmen (boosting the total number of witnesses to 114). These were "salt of the earth kind of people," Laurel Weir said.[8]

Weir compared the government's attempt to gain information on the Klan by infiltrating its ranks to the Russian system of "neighbors informing on neighbors." The defense even found two Negroes who testified of Sam Bowers's being "a good man" and a "very nice person" (in exchange for a crisp hundred-dollar bill, rumor had it).[9] The defense lawyers rounded up enough people to give alibis for thirteen of the eighteen defendants. The day of the killings, June 21, 1964, had been a Father's Day, so witnesses were able to claim vivid recollections of their friends' and kinfolks' whereabouts. No one offered an alibi for Bowers.

Attorney Mike Watkins, a member of the Klan's defense team, delivered a plea to the jury that sounded more like a rationale for vengeance than a plea of innocence. "There is no doubt in my mind," he insisted, "that there is some inward national disease gnawing away at the heart of our country— marches, riots, COFO organizations, or whatever you want to call it." It's no crime to be in the KKK, he reassured fellow Mississippians, just as it's no crime to hate "outside agitators" who come here "telling us how to run our business." In fact, if it was a crime to hate Yankee troublemakers, there'd be 420,000 white people in the state guilty as charged. "Mississippians rightfully resent some hairy beatniks from another state visiting our state with hate and defying our people. It is my opinion that the so-called [civil rights] workers are not workers at all, but low-class riff-raff, misfits in our own land."[10]

Watkins described the government's case against the Klan as an effort to use "central power" to intimidate fairly decent Mississippi whites. He reminded the jury, as if anyone could ever forget, that the assistant U.S. attorney general sitting before them, this same John Doar, was "the same man who put James Meredith in Ole Miss," the much-reviled sledgehammer swing into the iceberg of Mississippi segregation.

The Justice Department's Doar relied heavily on the testimony of two paid informants, Jim Jordon and Delmar Dennis, both of whom gave detailed accounts of the murders and of Bowers's role as chief architect. "If you find these men are not guilty, you will declare the law of Neshoba County to be the law of Mississippi," Doar told the jury shrewdly. "Just as there was no doubt a plot [to murder Chaney, Goodman, and Schwerner]," Doar continued, playing the stereotype against its extreme, "there was no doubt that the law of Neshoba County participated."

Doar reconstructed the three men's fateful drive of June 21, 1964, using as many local witnesses as possible to fortify his case's credibility. A Mississippi state highway patrolman took the stand to talk about his role in the arrest. The jailer's wife described the men's incarceration in the Neshoba County jail. A Meridian policeman explained the recruiting procedures and organization of the Lauderdale County Klavern, and also recalled hearing plans of the murders from Klansmen Frank Herndon and Edgar Ray Killen. The FBI informant Delmar Dennis, a ranking member of the White Knights hierarchy, gave the court a firsthand account of the Klan's decision to go after Schwerner.[11] The murders were Sam Bowers's brainchild, Dennis confirmed. Bowers had emerged from the killings "gleeful" and "pleased." "It was the first time that Christians successfully planned and carried out the execution of a Jew," he had boasted afterward.[12]

The informant also produced a copy of a letter from Bowers to his inner circle. In the letter, written in the heat of the FBI's investigation, Bowers tried to disguise the details of the murder in a set of guidelines regarding a lumber transaction. But the real meaning was clear to Dennis. He read Bowers's memo: "My experience this morning convinces me that the Main Plant is in possession of all the information regarding our secret logging operation, due to the loose talk of some of our truck drivers, but that as far as FACTS are concerned, they have nothing of value for which they could sue us."[13] The letter was signed "Willoughby Smead, Esq."

Dennis shrugged off the defense attorney's claim that Bowers had taken a recent interest in timber sales. "Willoughby Smead is Sam Bowers. The letter is in code. The 'main plant' is the FBI and the 'big logging operation' refers to the murder of the three civil rights workers."[14]

Dennis's testimony was damaging and caused the defense to begin reaching for straws. Attorney Weir raised the issue of Mickey Schwerner's reputation as an atheist—not only an atheist but a communist atheist. Weir assumed falsely that the all-white jury would share his belief that a communist atheist was fair game. Weir went on to say that Schwerner had tried "to get young Negro males to sign statements that they would rape one white woman a week during the hot summer of 1964 here in Mississippi."[15] But Judge Cox wasn't having any of it. He refused all speculation concerning the civil rights worker's theological or philosophical views and called the rape comment "highly improper" and inconceivable in the case of Schwerner. The trial came to an end.

After closing arguments, the jury members remained in session for two days, several times declaring themselves "hopelessly deadlocked." Finally, on Friday, October 20, the shocking news broke. An all-white Mississippi jury had reached a guilty verdict on conspiracy charges. Not only was Bowers found guilty of conspiring to murder the three men, but six other Klan members were also convicted, Alton Wayne

Roberts and Deputy Cecil Price among them. Neshoba
County Sheriff Lawrence Rainey and seven other men, including the itinerant preacher Edgar Ray Killen, were acquitted.
The convictions marked the first time an all-white Southern
jury had carried out the sentencing of a Klansman, a bold and
unexpected denunciation of the long season of violence.

There was no reason to consider Judge Cox any less the
bigot he was before the trial. "They killed one nigger, one Jew
and a white man," he said later in an interview in the *Jackson
Clarion-Ledger*. "I gave them what I thought they deserved."[16]
But to his credit, even Cox had lost patience with the Klan
and the bad times heaped on the state. When court officials
informed him that Roberts and Price had joked outside the
courthouse that a good bombing might be just the thing to
keep the jury honest, he had the two Klansmen taken into
custody and held without bail. Five hundred and fifty sticks of
dynamite and blasting caps had been stolen from a military
warehouse at the beginning of the trial, and the judge was
steaming mad. With Roberts and Price sitting before him in
his chambers (both visibly shaken by the judge's new resolve),
Cox explained in no uncertain terms, "If you think you can intimidate this court, you are sadly mistaken. I'm not going to
let any wild man loose on a civilized society." Cox accused
them of "stupidity," "hopelessness," "anarchy," and threatening
the "unthinkable." "There isn't anybody on earth who can
frighten this court," the judge added.

The Neshoba verdict was celebrated far and wide as the
ending of an era. The families of the victims expressed their
appreciation for the jury's decision. James Chaney's mother,

who'd moved to New York City after her son's death, told reporters, "They did better than I thought they would do." The NAACP's John Morsell praised the prosecution and the jurors "who turned their backs on a hoary tradition to uphold the American idea of equal justice." Martin Luther King, Jr., said he was "pleasantly surprised," applauding the convictions as "a first step in a thousand-mile journey toward the goal of equal administration of justice in Mississippi." The *New York Times* described the verdicts as a "measure of the quiet revolution that is taking place in Southern attitudes—a slow, still faltering, but inexorable conversion to the concept that a single standard of justice must cover whites and Negroes alike."[17] Even Judge Cox himself piped in, again declaring to the world "we are not going to have anarchy down here." Attentive observers got a hint of an emerging new sentiment in the minds of many white middle-class Mississippians—the Klan as trash. Almost everyone seemed hopeful the verdict would go a long way toward making our state a more peaceful place to live. My father felt confirmed in his optimism about Laurel's promising future.

The White Knights' numbers had declined dramatically. By the end of fall 1967, the FBI reported 600 remaining members, which should have been a hopeful sign of better days ahead, compared with the 7,000 members who filled the Klan's ranks during its heyday in the summer of 1964.

But, in fact, there was little evidence of peace in the weeks following. As Bowers studied the matter (free while awaiting sentencing), he knew smaller numbers required more extreme measures. Over the next month and a half, violence saturated Laurel, even as the national media analyzed the causes of the Klan's demise. A local editorial writer surmised that the escalated violence was "retaliation against recent arrests and trials of Klansmen." In the late fall of 1967, the FBI agent running the Laurel bureau gave the district attorney's office a list describing more than 140 recent acts of violence and terror in the Jones County area alone.

With a hailstorm of convictions and trials raining down on him, with FBI agents some days outnumbering Jaycee lunchers at the Magnolia Motor Lodge or the Pinehurst Hotel, Bowers refused to slow down. Even when word came that he'd been given the maximum ten years in prison for the Neshoba murders, he sloughed that off with hopes of a lengthy appeal. He aimed to fight the battle until the bitter end.

Autumn 1967. The Mississippi nights were electric with fear.

In Mt. Olive, a white Baptist pastor who had refused the Klan's request to make a contribution to the annual Lottie Moon Offering was threatened with a drive-by shooting. Crosses were burned at his home and on the front lawn of the nearby church.

In the Delta, a carload of ministers working for the National Council of Churches was pulled to the side of the road by Klansmen and beaten with baseball bats and chains.

In Taylorsville, a white minister's wife was told in a late-night phone call that unless her husband allowed Klansmen to recruit in their church, she would be killed along with her two small children.

At Tougaloo College, a bomb took out the living room and kitchen of a theology professor, leaving one side of the house torn open like the face of a movie set.

In Collins, Sam Bowers and a young recruit named Thomas Tarrants were arrested on their way to "take care of" Ancie McLaurin, according to the report filed by night marshal Buster Lott. McLaurin was a Negro man accused of shooting a policeman in nearby Mt. Olive. In their possession was a fully loaded machine gun and two additional ammunition clips.

In Jackson, the home of Perry Nussbaum, rabbi of Temple Beth Israel, was blown to bits by explosives, nearly two months after his synagogue's newly constructed sanctuary had been bombed on September 18. The explosion destroyed the kitchen, the dining room, the living room, and parts of a bedroom. Miraculously, neither Rabbi Nussbaum, a vocal supporter of civil rights causes, nor his wife was harmed.

In Laurel, shortly after midnight on November 15, a dynamite explosion ripped through the parsonage of St. Paul's United Methodist Church. The pastor, the Reverend Allan Johnson, was one of Laurel's most distinguished black leaders and an active member of the Voters League in Mississippi. Leontyne Price grew up in the church and sang an annual Christmas concert to a standing-room-only crowd. The bomb had been placed in the carport of Johnson's red brick rancher, demolishing the family's new Ford sedan and buckling the roof into the kitchen. The impact of the concussion propelled the living room furniture, including a new grand piano, through a bathroom wall and leveled the dining room. The bedrooms where the husband and wife and four grandchildren slept were somehow spared devastation. "Except for the mercy of God," Johnson said, "I don't see how it was possible for us to keep from getting hurt. And if this had happened an hour earlier, it would have gotten my whole family. My babies were playing the piano about eleven o'clock."[18]

To compound matters, tensions among striking workers at the Masonite plant exploded in violence midfall. Two unions—one black, one white, representing the International Woodworkers of America—had coexisted more or less peacefully until the 1964 Civil Rights Act required the consolidation of the two unions in compliance with federal desegregation laws. The unintended result was the election of all-white IWA officers, since whites composed 75 percent of the Masonite workforce.

But in October 1967, separate bathroom and shower facilities were banned by the Ohio-based Masonite management. When Klan-friendly white union members called a strike protesting the plant's decision (demanding that black workers actually join them at the picket line), the company began hiring Negro laborers to replace the white strikers. District Attorney Chet Dillard, a tough, large-framed man feared by the Klan, described Masonite and the surrounding property as "a virtual war zone" between the union hall and the power plant. "The workers in the power plant erected a three-quarter-inch steel plate over the windows facing the union hall for their protection," Dillard said. "There were numerous acts of dynamite explosions, shootings at workers, and countless other acts of violence."[19] When a drive-by shooting on the plant property left a security guard dead just inside the Masonite fence, the Klansman arrested for the murder told the assistant district attorney, "I shot the guy's fucking brains out and then went and drank me a cup of coffee."

Warring factions would reach a labor agreement in the spring of 1968, but for the long months of the strike, Laurel lived constantly with the fear that a full-blown race war would erupt, any hour of any day.

The day after the November 15 bombing in Laurel, a hundred Negroes marched from Allan Johnson's smoldering parsonage twelve blocks to the City Hall. The Reverend Milton Barnes, one of Johnson's black ministerial colleagues and a local SNCC organizer, told the angry crowd: "In no uncertain terms are the Negroes going to take any more. We do not want a Detroit in Laurel, but we are at the end of our patience. We want to live in peace if the white people will let us. We have taken every kind of abuse and turned the cheek three times, but we will not take any more."[20] Barnes turned his attention to the white onlookers milling about and asked whether among them stood "yellowbellys and dirty dogs who do their cowardly acts under the edge of darkness." If so, he wished to serve notice. From this day on, he said, Laurel Negroes intended to do "whatever is necessary" to protect themselves and to bring the culprits to justice.

In response to the marching Negroes downtown and rumors that civil rights leaders from across the South were on

their way to lend support to the cause, my father and thirty
other local white ministers hastily drafted a resolution against
Klan violence, which was published on the first page of the
newspaper and circulated in mimeographed sheets around the
business district. The Jones County Ministerial Association, as
the group was called, encouraged all Laurelites "to calm in-
flamed passions, to demonstrate brotherly love in all their relationships and to unite in the name of Christ and His Church
in their efforts to see that no further acts of violence mar the
character of our communities."[21] The resolution called the
bombing an "unmitigated act of cowardice" and "a symptom of
the underlying animosities, hatreds, and prejudices that find a
place in our midst," and pledged support "to those who are
seeking to repair the damage done, both physical and mental;
and to those law enforcement agencies who are seeking to
maintain law and order and to see that the perpetrators of this
crime are brought to justice." My father had not signed the
resolution without concerns for his own safety. He also had
serious reservations about ecumenical cooperation. Baptists
believed in the full independence of the congregation to make
decisions about policies and doctrine—this was called congregational polity—and were by nature suspicious of interde-
nominationalism, seeing it as the slippery slope to a cheap
and weakened faith. But all the downtown ministers had
signed on—Bill Crosland at First Presbyterian, E. E. Samples
at First Methodist, Armistad Jones at St. John's. Good gra-
cious, even old Luther Slay himself, a hard-shell type from
over at Wildwood Baptist, located in a working-class neighborhood near the county hospital, had chimed in with his ap-

proval. So my father added his name to the signatures and, like most of the other pastors, earned himself a few late-night rings of the telephone—Bowers's tried and true "Number 1," a barking voice or a high-pitched laugh followed by a dead line.

Allan Johnson preferred a different response to the Klan bombing, resisting the tactics of demonstrations or the white ministers' resolution. Johnson was a forceful but moderating voice, never quite at home in organizations like SNCC or CORE—whose penchant for the dramatic he sometimes found sophomoric. Before moving to Laurel, he had once lashed out in anger at a group of movement leaders who'd trashed his Jackson church during a mass meeting. With a rifle in one hand and a Bible in the other, he told them, "I am sick and tired of all of you, and I want you to know you are not going to run over me and continue tearing up my church. I have collected whiskey bottles from my Sanctuary upstairs, I have caught couples upstairs in the 'act' and had to run them out, and I am going to say one more thing to all of you. You vomited on the floor and furniture upstairs and broke out several of my windows and if I hear any more shooting at my church I will be the one doing it."[22]

Aside from an occasional need to clear the temple of the moneychangers, Johnson's work toward Negro improvement had followed the long, patient lead of the Southern Christian Leadership's Negro Voters League. He'd earned a reputation as an eloquent preacher and a leader in the United Methodist Church. But all that didn't really matter, his moderation and patience, when it came to dealings with the white thugs down the road. The Johnson family had many times been the target of late-night phone calls, honking horns, and catcalls. Earlier in the fall, shotguns were fired from a speeding car on Interstate 59, which cut through the neighborhood on elevated piers.

Johnson's response to the bombing was nothing short of genius. He invited Martin Luther King, Jr., to speak from his pulpit. And Dr. King, who had never before been to Laurel, accepted for a date in early spring.

On March 15, 1968, Reverend Johnson and his family hosted a meal for the civil rights leader in the restored parsonage. Ralph Abernathy, Hosea Williams, Dorothy Cotton, and Leon Hall, all members of the SCLC team, shared the table. In the sanctuary at St. Paul's later in the day, King lamented the moral state of our country, a spiritual wasteland in need of renewal, an America "where houses have wall-to-wall carpet" while too many others have "wall-to-wall rats and roaches." While no one recalls whether King drove the oak-lined streets of the historic district before arriving at the church, his speech captured the essence of the town's divided world.

King had come to Mississippi to promote the June camp-in on the Washington Mall, part of his Poor People's Campaign to bring attention to America. And like many of his final speeches, his words in Laurel were singed with a prophet's anger. "We're going to Washington to demand—not to beg— that something be done immediately to improve the lives of our poor people. We need jobs. We need jobs that will pay us something. We're tired of working on full-time jobs for part-time wages." Two weeks later, on April 4, 1968, Dr. King was murdered in Memphis.[23]

White Laurel would not be grieving over the slain civil rights leader. On Friday, the day after the murder, the playing fields at Mason Elementary were abuzz with reports of the shooting. "That nigger asked for it," said Boss Jones, a boy who had failed two grades and smelled like smoked pork. He was standing at the foul line getting set for an underhanded free throw. "My daddy said it's a good thing he's dead," said Clay Malone, as he reached over and whacked the ball out of Boss's hands. Billy Franklin, the son of a golf pro, said he wished they'd shoot Hubert Humphrey too. But the basketball game was already degenerating into a savage melee, half tackle football, half kamikaze rage, and soon the semideflated ball was replaced by pine branches and chunks of clay.

My parents, like most of their friends in town, were concerned about the "bands of Negroes, enraged over the murder of Martin Luther King, Jr.," who had already "burned, looted and clashed with police" in cities as close by as Memphis, Jackson, and Itta Bena. The *Laurel Leader-Call* had led off its coverage of the assassination with grave concern about revolution in the streets. "Racial Violence Racks Nation: Rampaging, Mobs Burn, Loot, Kill," read the headlines. "A white youth was suffocated in a firebombing in Tallahassee, an elderly man died in a fire in Harlem, and a white man died Friday of injuries suffered in the Washington violence," we were told. Still, it was comforting to know that even with King dead (and at the hands of a white drifter, we would soon learn), "metropolitan ghettos" and "Negroes heaving rocks and curses" were the real sources of American's race problem. Under the startling photograph—grim images of Negro rioters smashing store windows in the nation's capital—was the sole article about the association. "Best Known CR Leader," the piece was titled. "King himself was in jail more than a dozen times in seven years. He often led demonstrators clad in blue jeans and a denim jacket," concluded the summary of the civil rights leader's life and legacy.

Laurel remained peaceful in the wake of King's death. The revival set to begin on Friday at First Baptist Church proceeded as scheduled. Evangelist Eddie Hurt, who sported designer clothes and a dramatic swirl of blond hair, moved many in the audience to walk the aisle after his sermon "Rewards in Heaven." "The righteous man will not receive rewards in heaven for the works that he does," Hurt preached, "but for the crowns he wears." He meant the "Crowns of Bible study, personal soul-winning, faithfulness under trials, and Christian separation from the world." My father couldn't have been happier when a dozen people gave their life to Jesus each night of the three-day evangelistic crusade. Eddie Hurt's appeal to the life hereafter fell on fertile soil in that first week of April 1968.

10

Breather in the Big Easy

Throughout our first year in Laurel, I often begged my parents to take me to New Orleans. In my bedroom at night, with the shades drawn and the shutters latched, the darkness was vast and unrelenting and filled the room when the light was turned off. I could not fathom the choking fear that descended. Had it come from the devil, from the sinister forces alive in our Southern town, from some damage wrought by desire and fright? I dreamed strange dreams. A hard wind—thrusting open doors and windows—devoured the house, the walls, the spaces between, in sudden, overwhelming bursts. There was no hiding, no retreat. There was only a dark closing-in. New Orleans felt different.

My aunt and uncle lived there in a suburb called Gentilly, a neighborhood of failed colonial-style developments, ranchers, and white-washed apartment buildings—surrounded by po'boy stands, curb stores, and shopping centers. New Orleans was only a hundred and fifty miles from Laurel. If we left after breakfast, we could be sitting in the dining room of the Gumbo Shop by lunchtime. My parents were usually happy to oblige. My mother would call the assistant principal at Mason and tell her we were attending to family matters for the day. My father only had to call his secretary to rearrange his schedule and fill up the Impala.

Once past Hattiesburg, a university town twenty-five miles away, we had only the sparsely trafficked interstate and the sloping hills of the piney woods all the way to Picayune, the last town of any size before the Louisiana state line. The land became low and flat. In Picayune I put away whatever schoolwork I was doing and welcomed the strange world unfolding west of the Pearl River. We'd exit the interstate for a two-lane highway, bleached by the sun the color of shell, which seemed to carry us downward into a subterranean world of bayous and marshes. In warm weather, colonies of black skimmers and seagulls canvassed the coastal meadows on either side of the road. In winter, when the air was balmy and the gulf sky often overcast, the wetlands seemed immense, a world drifting seaward as though unlocked by floodwaters. The world had its own smells (fishy and sour) and tastes (like salted water). Ascending from the east bank of the Ponchartrain up the Highway 11 bridge with the city curving in the distance around the riverbank, I felt engulfed with happiness. Here was breakthrough: upward out of the backwater for this fat view of the city, and then down again into the middle of it all.

We drove to the French Quarter, no stopping or side trips along the way. There was never trouble getting a table at the Gumbo Shop on St. Peter Street (not in those days before the restaurant was discovered by the *New York Times*), and there was never any doubt about what to eat. Two dollars could get you a large bowl of gumbo, steaming with shrimp, sausage, oysters, and crab claws, and topped with a scoop of sticky rice, served with sourdough rolls and slabs of sweet butter. Dessert was pecan pie—pecans glazed with molasses and sugar in a dark brown mélange flavored with vanilla. Between courses I walked around the café and its shady courtyard. A wall-length mural of the Battle of New Orleans (fought in earnest after the War of 1812 had been decided) hung above the tables near the kitchen and gave the place a sense of whimsical motion. Between the dining room and the courtyard was a long, narrow bar, usually more filled than the restaurant.

After lunch I was free to stroll through the Quarter by myself, with a meeting place and time agreed upon. I'd visit the coin shops on Royal Street, buy a silver dollar or Indian-head nickel for my collection if I had the money. If not, I'd get a cheap bag of Mardi Gras doubloons. I'd also make a quick detour onto Bourbon Street, walking with my sights aimed straight away, hoping to appear to onlookers as a boy seeking his way to safer environs. But my plan was to swing into one of the souvenir shops and flip through the clunky files of posters, feasting in one exhilarating glance on the body of Barbarella or Raquel Welch in her *One Million Years B.C.* pose, or on any other of the graphic renderings of the New Morality—even though this obligated me before leaving to feign interest in some trinket or knick-knack, a toy monkey flipping somersaults or a Slinky, as if by attending however briefly to a wholesome diversion I had done small penance for my impure desires.

I'd head straight for Jackson Square after that, though I never seemed to get there the same way. Sometimes I'd approach from the south by Pirate's Alley and St. Anthony's Garden, sometimes from the east from Chartres and Wilkinson Streets. Even if I got momentarily lost, I'd sooner or later find myself on a tunnelway or sidewalk that opened onto the spacious piazza. Jackson Square was where the hippies gathered—Josh Seargroves everywhere you looked. I walked the perimeter of the park, taking in the sounds and sights and smells: guitar music echoing off the Cabildo; kids in dazzling, mismatched clothes, sitting on park benches and blankets. Strange smells filled the air: incense, cannabis, patchouli oil.

We would drive to Gentilly in the afternoon to visit my uncle Fortner, the theology professor at the Baptist seminary, and aunt Emily. While the adults sat at the kitchen table drinking coffee, I'd go with my younger cousins for a swim in the neighborhood pool, or if I could leave them at home, play basketball at the seminary gym. I loved the neighborhood, with its wide-open streets and white-shell sidewalks. Unlike Laurel with its heavy foliage and shady lawns, Gentilly lay be-

neath a huge sky. Sparse palms and palmettos gave it the sense
of an abandoned coastal plain.

In the evenings my father treated our relatives to dinner,
and the seven of us squeezed into the Impala and drove up
Gentilly Boulevard to Elysian Fields and then along Lakeshore
Drive with Ponchartrain Lake to our right. We always ate at
Fitzgerald's—a rambling mess of white shanties on stilts over
the lake. The specialty of the place was seafood, heaps of it,
fried in lard, in black vats, served on giant platters with french
fries and hush puppies. Tiny plastic cups of coleslaw were
pretty much the sole contributor of nutritional value, and
these were quickly discarded by me and my cousins to make
room for mounds of catsup, sometimes mixed together with
mayonnaise and a little horseradish to form a pink *rémoulade*.

In New Orleans, I felt free and alive, a long way away from
Laurel, that suffocating town, covered in a brown fog of violence. Years later I would remember these nights by the lake,
taking our dinner on the porch of the restaurant, beneath the
light of forty-watt bulbs, the air inside warmed by gas grates, a
breeze rolling across the invisible water, the soft dry sound of
the palm trees on the shore, my father, mother, and I happily
together. But, for now, our home lay two hours northeast up I-
59 in the piney woods of Jones County, and it was there we
would always have to return.

11

Local Assassin Makes Good

My father's big plans for a peaceful and prosperous vicarage were not going as scheduled. By January 1968, his hopes of creating a "significant church in a significant town" where an "on-fire people worshiped God and loved their neighbors" were being upstaged weekly by an on-fire Sam Bowers and his behooded crusaders.

That month, my father was invited to present the Jaycee Man of the Year award. He had developed a reputation as a crack after-dinner speaker, equipped with a wide repertoire of sports stories and humorous anecdotes, each containing a

pithy moral and brief though biting lesson in faith. His tiny
bathroom on the backside of our house—in an awkward addition used for a guest room—was a clutter of Sunday's *Clarion-
Ledger* sports pages, sermon manuscripts in progress, and soggy
issues of *Pulpit Digest*, from which many winning stories about
our family life in his sermons were loosely based. Although
the hobnobbing and the schmoozing did not come easily for
the once-stuttering boy from west Jackson, his twitchy constitution, his constant departures from the table to make a phone
call ("touching base" with his secretary, with Mom, or with
anyone else who came to mind), his keys jingling in his pants'
pocket like maraca beans, not to mention his excruciating
habit of ripping paper napkins with an ever-present hangnail,
all of this was more than offset by an exuberant kindness and a
fetching smile.

The winner of the Jaycee Man of the Year award was a
man named Clifford Wilson. Wilson's contributions to the
common good of south Mississippi primarily involved the
manufacturing of artificial limbs. But he had also been busy
with those activities that endear one to the larger public—
coaching little league baseball, heading up a Cub Scout pack,
hosting fund-raisers for various charitable causes, serving on
the PTA, keeping home and garden attractive, and otherwise
improving the world as best he could. He had once been
president of the local Jaycee chapter himself and was currently one of twelve area vice presidents of the Mississippi
branch.

My father was excited about the banquet. The Junior
Chamber of Commerce was promoting the event as the year's

first social gala. The mahogany walls and ornamented panels of the Masonite Room had been well burnished by the Negro help. The crystal chandeliers, the china, the silver place settings sparkled. Faith Harper was fast selling out of a new line of evening wear she'd selected for the occasion. Corum's Florist had prepared two hundred white carnation corsages for the ladies and red rose boutonnieres for the men. My father had even composed a new speech, "The Essence of a Good Community," and planned to sport a navy double-breasted suit with an oyster-white button-down he'd picked out at Hamilton James Men's Wear (a gift of appreciation from Nat James himself). When Chief of Police Harry Estep commented earlier in the day that something besides ham and peas would be served that night, my father smiled unknowingly and solicited his advice on some church matter.

"What can we do to have a good community?" my father asked the audience as they ate their apple cobblers and sipped coffee. Some smoked cigarettes.

"The essence of a good community is people like Clifford Wilson," he said, "people who relate to their fellow man and take an active interest in civic affairs, people who have a constructive influence on society, whose lives are driven by an intangible, invisible force that emanates from their personality."

My father said that the person who wants to be a constructive part of a good community must choose to live for more than himself. "People are realizing the questions of morality must be squarely faced," he explained. "The real problem is the way we sometimes treat the differences with indifferences."

The talk rambled around the edges of civil religion. America's problem was the absence of worthy goals; people who don't care for themselves, who don't respect others. "We need more men like Clifford Wilson—men willing to put the good of the community over their own interests and desires." There were palpable feelings of civic munificence in the ballroom, appreciation for my father's remarks, for the fine time shared by all, for the town's bright future, darkened for a spell by the events of the past few years but now, everyone hoped, behind us all.

Wilson accepted the bronze plaque, thanking the pastor for his inspiring words, the Jaycees for the honor, the business community of Laurel for its commitment to excellence. He promised to continue serving the people of Laurel to the best of his ability. He also asked for the audience's support next month as he traveled to Jackson as the town's nominee for Mississippi's Outstanding Young Man of 1967. My father was presented a copy of *The Jaycee Story*, along with a certificate of appreciation. The handsome young preacher and the venerable maker of artificial limbs were photographed exchanging handshakes and smiles. Within an hour, the FBI arrested Clifford Wilson, along with Sam Bowers and ten other local Klansman, for killing a black man named Vernon Dahmer.

Newspapers across the country reported the next morning that Clifford Wilson had been the White Knights' hit man in the firebombing death of Vernon Dahmer two winters earlier.[1] He was also identified as the president of the Mississippi chapter of the Americans for the Preservation of the White Race.

In January of 1966, just months after invoking the Fifth Amendment during the House Un-American Activities Committee's hearings on racist violence in America, Sam Bowers had ordered a "number 3 and a number 4" on Vernon Dahmer (a burning and a killing in Klan lingo). Vernon Dahmer was a prosperous landowner and businessman who had told parishioners at his church the night before the raid that they could pay their poll taxes at his general store, sparing themselves the trip to the county courthouse—where they'd be greeted by a circuit clerk who'd likely won his job after assuring whites he could keep the Negroes in line. Dahmer even offered to cover for those poor blacks who could not afford the tax. He lived with his family on a farm in the Kelly Settlement, ten miles outside of Hattiesburg between the Eatonville and Leaf Rivers.

Listen to Klan informant Billy Roy Pitts's account of the Dahmer killing and the "active interests" of Laurel's Man of the Year.

> We continued driving and crossed over an overpass that went over Interstate 59. We drove down a gravel road and passed a house which Sessum identified as the house we were to burn. We continued driving a short distance until we came to a church. Clifford Wilson drove into the church yard and the Ford pulled up alongside us. Then the Ford left with its group to make another pass by the house to ensure that everything was clear. It returned a short time later. I again expressed concern to Cecil Sessum and he told me to stop worrying, that Sam Bowers and Devours Nix were close by in the event that anything went wrong.

While both cars were in the church yard the other men began to get ready by putting on gloves and checking their weapons and the jugs of gasoline. I did not have any gloves and did not wear any.

When all was ready, both cars pulled out with the Pontiac leading. Both cars extinguished their lights prior to arriving at the Dahmer house. On arriving, Wilson drove up into the yard of the residence. Bill Smith and Cliff Wilson jumped out and immediately began firing into the house repeatedly. I recall that Wilson was shooting an automatic shotgun and Smith a pump shotgun.[2]

When he had finished firing shots from the yard, Clifford Wilson, flanked by his killing partners, ran to the front of the house with gasoline-filled jugs punching holes in the plastic sides with a knife. The men lobbed the jugs above the shrubbery through the picture window on the front porch, along with forked sticks enshrouded with gasoline-soaked rags lighted with matches. Soon the front part of the house was engulfed in flames.

As the house burned, Klansmen sprayed gunfire into the windows and onto the porch, where Dahmer appeared with his shotgun. "Jewel, get the children out while I hold them off," he told his wife. But the outside doors were already consumed in flames, as was the hallway from the front of the house to the back. Mrs. Dahmer managed to get out by ramming her shoulder against a back bedroom window until she broke through to the frost-covered ground below. Ten-year-old Bettie Dahmer suffered severe burns on her head and arms; the other children at home that night, Harold, who was twenty-six, and eleven-year-old Dennis, were able to reach

cover unharmed. Dahmer's eighty-four-year-old aunt Lurian-
nie Heidelberg escaped through the back door of the general
store, where she had been sleeping in the back room. However, Vernon Dahmer, standing guard on the front porch, firing his shotgun into the violent assault, inhaled fatal lungfuls
of smoke and flame. "He was shooting back all the time," his
wife recalled later at the trial. Vernon Dahmer died the next
morning in a Hattiesburg hospital, although he managed to
drive his family to a hospital in Hattiesburg before collapsing.

Klansman Billy Roy Pitts had taken part in the plot to kill
Dahmer, but in the fall of 1967 had signed a lengthy affidavit
giving FBI agents the details they needed to proceed with arrests and trials. His testimony continues:

> We ran back to the Pontiac. Bill Smith got into the rear seat,
> Cecil Sessum gone [sic] into the middle front seat, I gone into
> the right front seat on the outside. Wilson was driving. As Wil-
> son started to pull out of the yard, I observed the store burning.
> In the light I could see the other car parked. Bill Smith saw the
> other car and apparently thinking it was someone else, Smith
> opened fire on the car with his pump shotgun. . . . I yelled at
> Smith and asked him what was the matter with him. I don't recall
> exactly what he said but it was something to the effect that he
> thought it was somebody else.
>
> Wilson sped out of the yard and down the road, followed by
> the other group in the Ford. . . . It was obvious the Ford could
> not keep up so both cars stopped together. We discussed burn-
> ing the Ford but discovered we had no gasoline left.
>
> About this time, I discovered that my pistol was gone from
> the holster. . . . Everyone was concerned about this but we de-
> cided we could not go back and get it. . . . We abandoned the

Ford alongside the road and everyone continued on to Cecil Sessum's house in Wilson's Pontiac.

On more than one occasion since the Dahmer burning, Sam Bowers has personally cautioned me to keep my mouth shut and stated that if any member of the group ever dealt with the government, they would get the hell beat out of them. Bowers also told me that if anyone pimped on the deal, the pimp would hang with the others.[3]

FBI agents were surprised by the wide trail of evidence left behind—the abandoned getaway car, the lost weapon—leaving them to speculate on the quantities of whiskey or narcotics consumed for the mission.

My father did not hear the news of Wilson's arrest until he was going to bed. Police Chief Harry Estep, who was also a parishioner at First Baptist, called with the report. As was his custom at the end of the day, my father was in bed with the week's sports pages spread out beside him. He listened to Estep and tried to fit the facts together.

Clifford Wilson's firm, Laurel Brace and Limb, was an entirely different operation from Bowers's Sambo Amusement Company. His uptown pretensions notwithstanding, Bowers made his home in south Mississippi's redneck underworld, which catered to the patrons of juke joints, truck stops, and trailer park lounges. His personal assistant, Devours Nix, ran a greasy spoon that served Jax beer and corn dogs. Manley Purris, a Klan attorney and indicted kidnapper, was an outright sociopath, violent even to his own kin. His son Bookey a classmate of mine at Mason, came to school with bruises and burns on his skin, dressed in tatters. The Roberts brothers, Alton Wayne and Raymond, indicted coconspirators in the Neshoba murders, owned a creepy nightclub on the outskirts of Meridian that was known to be a gathering place for "nigger-knockers" and country whores. And these were some of the Klan's class acts.

But Clifford Wilson? He was one of us, the kind of man you'd invite to your cookouts on summer evenings, want on your softball team. His children swam at the country club pool, went on church hayrides, vacationed in the panhandle of Florida. His Laurel Brace and Limb occupied a handsome brick building in the medical complex near the interstate. Perhaps there were a few peculiarities in his character later mulled over by friends and associates. He had a hard time looking people in the eye. At times he seemed downcast and preoccupied, and in general, he comported himself like a disheveled fraternity boy. But no Jaycee member or businessman in town would have ever believed the FBI agent who called Wilson "a model of propriety by day" and "a terrorist at night."[4]

"I feel like a fool," my father said.

"We're all fools," Estep replied. "The whole town's a fool. Nobody gets out of this looking good."

"What should I do?"

"No one who knows you would ever think you're pro-Klan. The media will say whatever it wants. There's nothing you can do about that. You just didn't know. The FBI had been working the case for months, but I was sworn to secrecy. I am sorry I couldn't have told you more before the banquet."

"I'm sorry, too," my father said.

"Look, you're a good man, Bob. We're solid people here—most of us anyway. We'll get through this just fine. I'll bet you one thing though. I bet Sam Bowers is having himself a good laugh right now."

"You think he had anything to do with this?"

"Who knows? He seems to think we're all pawns in his game."

"I've completely embarrassed myself and the church," my father said after a pause.

"Look, please try not to be hard on yourself right now. We've had a difficult night. But this is not the end of the world. Save those thoughts for the morning."

"Myra's afraid all the time. It doesn't matter how much I tell her everything's okay. I get the phone hung up on me at least once a week. My son has nightmares. One of his friends called the other night and told him he'd kidnapped me. He disguised his voice with a pillow or something. His momma let him have it when she found out. But Charles believed every word of it."

"I know it's tough. It's tough on all of us," Estep said. "But I can assure you things are going to get better soon."

"In the meantime, the pastor of the First Baptist Church is handing out awards to cold-blooded killers."

"Goodnight, Bob."

My father put the receiver down and walked into the kitchen. My mother was standing at the sink, washing dishes. She turned slowly around to face him.

"I'm so sorry, Bob," she said. "I know you must feel like screaming."

"I don't know what to do," he said, looking through the kitchen window into the well-lighted side yard. "I'm going to get calls from newspapers all over the place. What am I going to say for myself? They won't believe for one minute I was ignorant of the whole mess. And what hurts me so much is that one thing I've always taken great pride in is having some integrity about the race issue. It looks real bad, you gotta admit."

"There are so many pressures in Laurel," my mother said. "But the people in this church love you, they really do. You are their shepherd, their kind and loving shepherd, and they are going to take care of you."

"I was so excited about coming to this town," my father answered. Andalusia was a terrific place, but Laurel was the call I'd been waiting for. Back in our home state, in a super church, the opportunity of a lifetime. You know what I mean. I haven't even been here five months and look at me. I'm worn out, and I don't know how much more I can take."

Early the next morning, my father sat down at the kitchen table and wrote a letter to Dr. Leo Edwards, the seminary president in New Orleans. He told Dr. Edwards that he'd prayerfully considered the matter and felt God was calling him to the academic life. Were there any openings in the seminary faculty? He'd be real interested if there were.

A few weeks later my father was steering the Impala into the seminary's VIP parking lot on Gentilly Boulevard. Edwards had written back that he was pleased to hear of Bob Marsh's interest in a teaching post. The dour New Testament scholar had never regarded my father's intellectual skills as anything more than average, but he was impressed by the young preacher's dedication to the church. Although there were no jobs available in systematic theology or Biblical studies, positions normally filled with men holding European degrees, there was an opening in Christian education. The salary would never match what he made in a church like First Baptist, and he'd lose many of the perks he'd come to enjoy—the spacious pastor's study, the full-time secretary, the car allowance, the travel account, the book budget, and the country club membership. But the seminary would hire him with tenure and give the family a newly built colonial-style home on campus. There were other benefits too, like the use of a retreat house in Biloxi, a sabbatical program he'd never have as a preacher, and summers free for research and travel. There was a good public school on Franklin Avenue where most of the seminary children went. Edwards also showed my father plans for the new Christian-ed complex, built in the same French provincial architecture as the older buildings. We could move as early as summer if we wanted.

My father hurried back to Laurel after the meeting—pausing briefly at the po'boy stand across the street for his usual shrimp boat and Barq's. Driving back into the piney woods of south Mississippi in the fading winter light, he felt a big burden of worries slide off his back. It was true he had always been cool to the idea of raising a child in New Orleans—too many bad influences, too many Catholics. He'd never really liked seminary, hadn't cared much for the professors or the nitpicky theologians with their pipes and Paul Tillich. (The Baptist seminary was still decades away from a fundamentalist coup d'état that would send the liberals packing.) Of course, he'd read a little Tillich himself, sprinkled some of his phrases around—"ground of being," "ultimate concern," were there others?—cited him in his dissertation for the sake of the advisers; and then he heard about the foot fetish, the fondness for porn, the erotic stampedes. Lands alive, he wouldn't read Tillich now for all the rice in China. (What is a "ground of being," anyway?)

But now my father felt himself coming to a new perspective on the matter—not on Tillich but on the possibilities of academe. He'd matured, developed a fresh set of expectations, become more disciplined in his studies of the church.

When he got home, he told my mother to put the dinner in the freezer. We were going to Chandler's for steaks.

His mood was positively luminous. He wanted to know all about me. How school was going. What I was reading. Who my friends were.

I told him Jimmy Cooper had called me a bastard on the playground, and he didn't seem fazed at all.

"Next time that happens, you know what you should do?"

I was listening.

"Call him a lettuce head."

"A what?"

"A lettuce head. Kind of like beating him at his own game but not really. I bet he won't know what hit him." He called to the waiter. "Give this boy the biggest steak in the house."

"I'll have a hamburger, please," I said.

"And just leave that pot of coffee right here on the table, if you don't mind," he said.

My mother smiled. She would indulge him one quick fling with the notion before reminding him that no child of hers would be raised in New Orleans, Louisiana. Her point might be phrased in the idiom of female submissiveness—"God has yet to lay that vision upon my heart"—but the meaning was the same: not until hell freezes over, sweetheart.

He didn't actually talk about the job at dinner. My only clue that something was up came during the blessing. Even though I was not even a teenager yet, I'd already acquired the preacher kid's knack for discerning the serious amid the ordinary, for decoding the cryptic grammar of God-speak, especially when my welfare was at stake. He reached for our hands (indicating an emotional intensity beyond the normal) and bowed his head. "Lord, we're so thankful for this time together, for this food and for the exciting opportunities for ministry you've given us. Please help us know your will for our lives; and please make us open to your guidance. In Jesus' name, amen."

Trust me, there was trouble brewing.

My mother hardly had time to make her case against child rearing in the Big Easy. A phone call came in unexpectedly from the president of the Southwestern Baptist Theological Seminary in Ft. Worth. Would my father consider a homiletics post there?

Why certainly, he exclaimed, flooded by a happiness as thick as a thunderstorm. A Continental Airlines flight to Texas was followed by another teaching offer, but this time in a more family-oriented city where Baptists outnumbered Catholics two to one and streets had normal names.

One immediate effect of my father's sudden popularity on the academic market was an inflated sense of courage in the face of the prevailing Klan terror. *L'affaire Wilson* had shaken his pastoral confidences, awakened him to the fact that Mississippi burning could not be stashed away in some ecclesial nook and cranny. It also got him a manila envelope from his mother, sans greetings or note of any kind, stuffed with news clippings from the Jackson paper informing readers of communist agents dressed in the vestments of compassion and mercy. Liz Marsh had recently surprised her optimist husband and their bridge partners and become an active member of St. Columbo's Episcopal Church, a church holding firmly to the belief "that the various races in the United States can best achieve their maximum development and the protection of their racial integrity by resisting all attempts at mongrelization." The Sovereignty Commission named Liz and the other founding members "The Terrible 73"—as in "terrible swift sword"—marching as it did to the drumbeat of the "King James Bible, the Book of Common Prayer and its independence from the Protestant Episcopal Church in the United States," resisting "the national church's swing toward socialism."

By the end of March, with the two offers in hand, and—God be praised, when it rains it pours!—a pulpit committee coming some Sunday soon from the Metropolitan Baptist Church of Washington, D.C., my father experienced an exhilarating burst of moral energy. The old anxieties pervading his thoughts disappeared. He felt empowered to ascend the strategic pulpit of First Baptist and speak against the day. "I have to make clear to people near and far that the KKK does not truly represent the faith of our Lord," he wrote in his journal. "I have to take a more categorical stand against the Klan." He also decided to call on Laurel's best-known preacher-activist and tell him about his new resolve.

Marcus Cooley was the pastor of the Morning Side Tabernacle in the heart of the Queensburg neighborhood. The black Baptist church had opened its doors to COFO and SNCC in the first days of the 1964 Summer Project—and paid the price with drive-bys and burning crosses. For reasons he couldn't quite put his finger on, my father had always felt uncomfortable in Cooley's presence. The Negro pastor's demeanor somehow registered a slight demurral to the widely established fact of my father's ministerial preeminence.

He asked Cooley if he could visit him in his church office. (The burst of moral energy did not include a biracial lunch at the Manhattan Café.)

He said that was fine. Come on by.

Cooley might have wished his white pastor colleague had picked a better afternoon for a visit, whatever it was he wanted to talk about. Cooley had let a church member who owned a barbershop try out a new hairstyle on him, a kind of proto–Al Sharpton perm that draped over his scalp like peat moss. Cooley explained that his deacons had talked him into it, saying he needed a new image. The two Baptist preachers shared a laugh, and my father admitted that his deacons had said more or less the same thing, only they thought he should stop jogging around town in dirty jerseys and sweatpants.

After the church secretary served the pastors coffee, my father began speaking.

"Brother Cooley, I'm here to tell you some really good news. I know you've been critical of the white pastors in town. You don't think we've done enough to help the Negroes, and, you know, you're probably right about that. But what I want to tell you today is that as far as I am concerned all that's going to change from here on out." He reached into his pocket for evidence, beaming a proud smile.

"You know what I have here?" he continued. "I have letters from two different seminary presidents offering me teaching jobs. And do you know what that means?"

The Negro pastor smiled faintly.

"That means I am free." My father let the words come out slowly. "Free at last, I guess you could say. I'm free to do what's right, because I no longer have anything to lose. This means I can finally get up in the pulpit and speak about the race issue, about those things you and your people are concerned with, and I don't have to worry about what happens. If I lose my pulpit, I'll still have these offers in my hand."

Marcus Cooley was well versed in the subtleties and pitfalls of Southern racial etiquette. He knew how to navigate the rhetorical waters as well as anyone. He tried—mostly with success—to restrain himself during the various biracial clergy gatherings he always found patronizing and offensive. But my father's remarks made him mad. Through the east window of his office, he could see the ruins of the Freedom House, bombed so many times it finally waved the white flag in defeat, and beyond that the elevated stretch of the interstate from where Klansmen routinely fired shotguns on the Negro homes below. He was tired of handshakes and promises, tired of feigned gratitude.

"I understand what you're getting at," Cooley said. "I really do. And I appreciate your coming here today. But, Dr. Marsh, the truth is you're not free at all. You have no idea what free means."

Cooley leaned forward in his seat and rubbed his forehead with both hands.

"A man isn't free when he takes a stand because he has nothing to lose," he said. "Surely you understand this. Surely you understand that until you are willing to lose everything, you will never know what it means to be free."

My father's smile vanished. He felt as if the wind had been knocked out of him, and after a few false starts, he told Cooley he hadn't meant to say he wasn't willing to make sacrifices. He just wanted to tell him he was ready to lend a hand.

The black preacher laughed softly.

"Dr. Marsh, Vernon Dahmer was a friend of mine. He left behind a wife and eight children. Their lives will never be the same. You gave one of his killers the Man of the Year award a few weeks ago, and now you expect me to think you care about justice."

"I didn't know anything about Clifford Wilson. Nobody did. You know that. In a million years, I wouldn't have knowingly done such a thing. I am absolutely ashamed about that, but I can't change what happened."

"And what have you done with that shame? Have you told your people to support the law of the land? Have you told them that racism is a sin against God? Have you told them black people should have the same rights as whites? What have you done with that shame?"

My father returned the letters to his pocket. He was now getting rather mad himself. *Slow down, boy,* he thought.

But the Negro pastor wasn't finished. He pulled a copy of Martin Luther King's "Letter from Birmingham City Jail" off the bookshelf and began reading aloud. Cooley had picked a passage on the hypocrisy of white Southern clergymen who cautioned patience while violence raged unchecked. My father couldn't believe what he was hearing.

"I have been gravely disappointed with the white moderate," Cooley read. "I have almost reached the regrettable conclusion that the Negro's great stumbling block in the stride toward freedom is not the white Citizens' Councilor the Ku Klux Klanner, but the white moderate who is more devoted to 'order' than to justice; who prefers a negative peace which is the absence of tension to a positive peace which is the presence of justice; who constantly says, 'I agree with you in the goal you seek, but I can't agree with your methods of direct action'; who paternalistically feels that he can set the timetable for another man's freedom; who lives by the myth of time and who constantly advised the Negro to wait until a 'more convenient season.' Shallow understanding from people of good will is more frustrating than absolute misunderstanding from people of ill will. Lukewarm acceptance is much more bewildering than outright rejection."[5] That pretty much summed up Bob Marsh, Cooley seemed to be saying, pausing in his reading.

He would have continued, but my father interrupted him. "Why don't we get together again sometime soon and pick this up then. I've got to get on back to the church now. I do thank you for the chance to talk, though."

"That's fine, Dr. Marsh," Cooley replied. "But let me just say one more thing before you go. I'm a Mississippian like you, a preacher in the Christian church like you. Not only that, my father was a preacher, and so was his father before him. The last time our church was bombed, my son asked me where God had been when the Klansmen showed up. You know what I told him? I said, 'Child, don't be afraid. God will never leave you or forsake you. God will always calm the stormy waters. He did it two thousand years ago, when the disciples were fearful and the master stretched out his hand, and he will do it today.' You know what that boy did? He put his head on my shoulder and started crying.

"Now the thing is, I'm not sure I know what that means anymore. I'm not sure I'm really able to say that by my own lights. But when I saw the fear in my son's eyes, I just fell back on the one thing a Negro pastor in this town has to say—what he'd better say if he's going to be able to look himself in the mirror. And it was kind of like God talking to us.

"Dr. Marsh, my question to you this afternoon is, When are you going to start listening?"

Driving up 4th Avenue back to the church, my father felt his senses jangling, his emotions too much alive, fitful. He drove the streets of the Negro quarter, where men and women were walking to their houses in the pale light. He saw a small boy in a Spiderman jersey run his bicycle off the sidewalk and two older boys come to his aid. He saw an old woman wearing a bandanna pulling a hot tamale cart and a man standing over a campfire in the corner of an empty lot. He passed the local headquarters of the NAACP, housed in a sparsely supplied clothing store, every aperture of the window covered with sheets of plywood; the COFO House, long since boarded up and abandoned; the skeletal remains of the *Chronicle*, once the town's distinguished Negro weekly; and the darkened windows of East Jerusalem Baptist Church at the corner of 4th and Poole. The neighborhood looked worse than exhausted; it looked embattled, ruinous.

My father had been challenged point-blank by the Negro preacher to do better. "Cooley's response sent shock waves over me," he wrote to me in a letter many years later. "I was angry and I was humiliated. I felt like a balloon when you stick a needle in it, a lot of noise coming to nothing."

Back in his study, my father closed the curtains and sat in his leather chair. On his desk, a four-tiered photograph frame sat next to the Freedom Medal and a white marble block with his name engraved in black—"Dr. Bob Marsh." The four photos were of me, at age six, taken at a studio in Montgomery. In the first frame from the left, I'm staring directly into the camera, my chin arched forward according to instructions. In the second, my face is lit up in a big smile, a rare moment of unguarded delight, my snaggled front teeth visible for the world to see. In the third frame, I am looking to the right of the photographer. I seem surprised. My eyes are wide open, and on my head a cowlick in the back is ungluing itself from my mother's brushing. In the fourth frame, the photo is in profile, my eyes are puffy in the manner of a child's early-morning tenderness, and I'm looking slightly upward as if awaiting a word from someone, from my father, not sure what will be asked but trusting all the same.

Here he was. Thirty-five years old. He had a doctorate in hand—an Ed.D. earned the old-fashioned way, with course-work, comps, and dissertation, not the new mail-order variety gaining popularity among Southern preachers. The diploma had been matted in an oak and gold-gilded frame and hung on the wall above his other degrees—the B.A. from Baylor, the bachelor's of divinity, the master's of religious education. He had all he could ask for: good health, a wife who satisfied his needs, a growing and obedient son. His career was taking off; everywhere he traveled people regarded him as an up-and-coming preacher in the loquacious Southern tradition. He had the job offers from the seminaries, the search committee on the way down from the nation's capital, speaking invitations convention-wide, boards of trustees to serve on.

The frenzied events of the previous fall, the FBI agents rounding up suspected murderers and terrorists all over town, cast a dark shadow over Laurel's future and, now, it seemed, his own. For the first time, my father began to think, reluctantly, aggravatingly, that there might be blood on his hands too. He could no longer pretend that the main source of the Southern crisis was the two-faced clergy of the National Council of Churches, the outside agitators, the communist organizers, the beatnik priests. In recent months, he had paid lip service to the popular sentiment that Klan violence should be condemned because it threatened the traditional race relations in Mississippi. "I am against race mixing," my father told his deacons, "but we must do something to stop the violence and uphold the law." After a while, however, condemnation of this sort seemed not so much different from denial itself. It was "disidentification," as some historians would later call it, inculpability in the form of pointing the finger at the all-too-obvious villains slurping coffee at the Admiral Benbow Coffee Shop.

Most white people were fed up with the Klan. More than one Northern industry had hightailed it out of our bomb-drenched Jones County in the past couple of years. Small-town dailies editorialized against them as a matter of course, taking a stand for law and order. Disidentification served the useful purpose of pushing the white terrorists so far beyond the pale of civilized society that there was no need to accept blame for their evil deeds. They were crackers, rednecks, hillbillies, hicks, trailer trash, lint heads, swamp rats, lunatics. Anything but us. But with that said, there was no need to question the everyday practices of white supremacy. You could make your annual Christmas mission of mercy to poor Negro families and your resolutions against "unmitigated cowardice" without fear of unsettling the fragile balance of separate but equal. You could go on strutting through the world with a patrician's confidence, with the belief that the time-honored ways of the South represented civilization's finest achievement.

But alone in his office, face to face with the expanding credentials of success, my father knew what he really was.

He was a coward. Marcus Cooley had pointed a finger at everybody's favorite preacher and told him he was part of the problem. He was a hypocrite. Marcus Cooley had pointed out the audacity of thinking that bags of food and clothes at Christmas time were enough.

No, resolutions against Klan violence or for money to train Negro ministers were not even close to adequate recompense for the cruel centuries, the dark passage, the Southern Way of Life.

My father knew in his heart that Cooley was right. He knew that the Bible strained people's sights toward a New Kingdom—and one that lay a long way from the big mess he had on his hands in south Mississippi. He knew his own ministry stood under the judgment of the God he served. And yet knowing this only made all the more poignant the conclusion that he still could not preach about race. He couldn't see himself acting any differently. "I felt guilty and confused; sometimes paralyzed by fear, other times by all the built-in ideas about racial separation. I did not know what to do. But I also did not want to ruin our lives."

What he meant was that had he assumed the role of Atticus Finch, B.D., we would have been run out of town by sundown. When my father confided in a deacon one day at lunch that he was ashamed of himself for getting involved in the Wilson debacle, and frustrated that he had not known what was up, the man replied, "It's a pity about that Dahmer nigra, but you can't say he didn't ask for it." In the past couple of years, dozens of Mississippi preachers had lost or quit their Mississippi pulpits for voicing support of federal civil rights laws, for advocating open-door policies in the church, or just for waffling platitudes on equality. In 1963, twenty-eight young Methodist ministers had drafted a declaration called "Born of Conviction," affirming the belief that "Jesus Christ . . . permits no discrimination because of race, color or creed." By summer's end, sixteen of them had been forced to resign. By 1967, only seven of the twenty-eight signatories had been spared their congregations' wrath. Most of these ministers, like my father, would never have joined a civil rights organization. Their convictions were simple, taken from the Bible in plain and literal trust. "In Christ Jesus, you are all sons of God, through faith." "God is no respecter of persons." But time and again the simple lesson proved cause for dismissal. "They tried heaping vile on me," said one defrocked preacher, "with taunts of 'nigger lover,' 'your wife and a nigger,' 'get him a nigger church,' and 'bet his son marries a nigger.'"[6] Resignation meant you were given the opportunity to publicly recant, "with strong emphasis on the fact that you would lose your home and job if you did not," though you would probably lose them even if you did. If you didn't recant, the church voted unanimously for dismissal, at which point you were urged never to show your face around these parts again.[7]

Baptists of our Southern stripe regarded the local church as the sole authority in all matters of Christian faith and practice. This was called "congregational polity," as mentioned earlier. Lots of books and articles have been written on the subject, and like any theological idea, congregational polity has its own complex history of controversy and dispute. Still, it's a pretty easy idea to summarize: If you are a Baptist preacher and want to be successful, you better size up the people quickly. If they want aqua carpet instead of the standard maroon, you'll take a sudden liking for the aqua. If they root for Ole Miss over the Crimson Tide, you'll not say too much about your fondness for the Bear. If they want you to keep quiet about Negroes, you'll put a lid on your uneasy conscience. No bishop or presbyter will come to your defense. The local church is free to do its own thing, governed by the contingencies of race, class, and custom, by whatever idiosyncrasies prevail. In the 1960s, congregational polity turned out to be the Southern Way of Life baptized by immersion.

What would the three of us do if my father got fired? Live in exile in some ecclesiastical Siberia in northern Illinois? Certainly we could move to New Orleans or Ft. Worth. But my father didn't want that. Preaching was all he wanted to do or felt called to. That's what kept it all together, kept the wheels turning, preaching, pastoring, shepherding his flock, not teaching or administrating. These were the things that gave his life meaning.

We could move to Washington, D.C., where the downtown congregation had integrated years earlier. But my father didn't want that—nor did we. We had flown up to the nation's capital and met the pulpit committee at the Metropolitan Baptist Church, and the trip was a disaster. We arrived at the Baltimore-Washington airport three hours late, landing in a heavy snow. My mother had been so distressed by the storm that she opened up her Bible, spread it across her lap, and began reading verses aloud as the plane made its bumpy descent over the

Chesapeake Bay. Then, at dinner, I told the chairman of the
deacons and his wife, while we were eating at a fancy restaurant on Connecticut Avenue, that I thought the steak tasted
kind of "beefy" (they politely agreed with me) and that the
parsonage we had all visited on the way to supper—a Cape
Cod in Bethesda on a busy intersection with wall-to-wall carpet and a master suite on the first floor—needed an overhaul.
My parents were so angry they wouldn't let me watch TV
when we got back to the hotel room. The next day at church,
the parishioner's son who was told to escort me to Sunday
School crammed his knuckles into my forehead when we were
alone and told me to keep my distance. Everyone in the class
made fun of my accent, even the overweight teacher who
talked about Moses leading the Israelites "oat" of Egypt. My
parents had fared no better. The trial sermon lasted too long
and contained a racially insensitive remark, at least this was
the opinion of a well-known Baptist leader in the church who,
first off, informed my father that Washingtonians won't stand
for twenty-five-minute sermons, being temperamentally more
"high church," and then corrected his use of the word "Negro."
My father had told the story of the Negro opera star Leontyne
Price—whose voice had been discovered by the wealthy
white matron whom her mother worked for in Laurel—as an
example of God's raising even the lowliest to high places. "You
should really know that 'black person' is the acceptable term
now," the man said. My father felt like running off to an empty
classroom and crying. My mother complained that the church
ladies lacked a certain warmth, that they didn't seem interested in her ideas about the role of the pastor's wife, and had

talked only about themselves. We decided to stay in Mississippi—could not have been happier when the Delta jet touched down on dry ground in Jackson—near Lillian Toler, near our friends, in the deep evangelical South. This was home.

There was once a time when I wished my father had done more, that he had emerged as a freedom fighter, learned life-changing lessons from the Negro preacher, rolled up his cotton shirtsleeves, and confronted the Wizard with his evil ways. When I was a student at Harvard, I made up a story along these lines. I had my father framed in the Wilson case, punishment for his civil rights crusading. Over beers with intellectuals in Cambridge, I would recall crosses burning in the front yard, hoodlums trampling through azalea beds, the knotted frays of dynamite, and my father, standing tall, armed with a baseball bat, a hammer, the souvenir tomahawk from Cherokee, North Carolina—with the Word of God! I had us fleeing Jones County, my father's conviction leading to our exile from Mississippi, unvanquished, proud.

But that's not the way it happened. His journal from the spring (written in single words or phrases in large, frantic stabs) is a bleak vista into his world's unmaking.

February 1968

—*so confused about it all . . . so discouraged in being a man of God*

—*all I desire is His will, His presence & power—that is ALL!*

—*dead day—feel so distressed, really tough, blah staff meeting, went running*

—*ate at home, rode bike, fell down, Charles flew kite, real distressed*

He declined the job offers, had second thoughts too late, and finally hung his hopes on a position in Columbia, South Carolina, that never materialized.

March 1968

—*cold day, walked with Myra, stayed home with Charles, real tired*

—*beautiful weather, walked & ran, really down about work here, good crowd for family night*

—*fantastic weather, dead day, we walked around cemetery, new members' reception dead*

—*came home early & walked, bed early*

—*why no peace?—I turn it all over to you, Lord*

Throughout the spring, there are "bad scenes" with my mother, shouts muffled behind the kitchen door, a plate smashed on the sink.

April 1968

—*all is flat and dead, ran in park, good crowd at prayer meeting*

—*beautiful weather, lunch at Captain Joe's, ran in Park, stayed home, defeated*

—*so discouraged about work*

—*horrible day, catfish with the Robertses*

—*so disappointed in myself, good crowd for Bible study*

—*deep disgust with myself, stupid, stupid.*

He took long naps in the afternoon, stared at the TV set after supper, and greeted my tugs for attention with a sneer that left me breathless. In the journals, I fare no better.

—*watched Charles practice baseball, no big deal there*

—*really struggling, flat . . . Charles sick in bed*

—*Charles's new bike had blow-out . . . WHY?*

—*Charles sick with rash*

—*nothing going on, ran in Park, Charles home sick*

—*Charles struck out three times, horrible dragging day*

He laughed when he heard I'd bought Kimberly Weeks an amethyst ring for her birthday. "You spent five dollars on that girl! You're eleven years old and you want to go steady. Don't tell me to be quiet, Myra."

During basketball games in the backyard, he trash-talked until my arms shook with rage. "Come on, wimp, try to drive on me." He waved his hands, danced around the concrete court. "You're psyched out, I can see it," he said, as my jump shot sailed wide of the rim. I wanted to hurt him back, tell him how pitiful his set shot looked, two-handed, flat-footed, like some farm boy from the days of black and white. If he was such a great athlete, where were his trophies? I'd seen his clarinet and band uniform. Why didn't he bring that out of the closet? Put on his busby and march around the block. That'd look real good, wouldn't it?

My father lost his nerve. He despaired, broke down. There was just too much happening too quickly.

The Klan trials for the murder of Vernon Dahmer had also just begun in Hattiesburg. The large turnout of national media was evident in the no-vacancy sign outside the Pinehurst Hotel, where journalists were staying in droves hoping to get a scoop on the Klansmen from some of the hometown folk. My father would be named in the book by Don Whitehead, *Attack on Terror: The FBI Against the Ku Klux Klan in Mississippi*, as the Baptist preacher who'd hailed the "youthful executive" as a model of Christian manhood.[8] But my father answered with a curt "No sir, I'm not doing that. Now please don't call again" when a defense lawyer for Clifford Wilson called him and asked him to testify for his client. "Most good people of Laurel did not really understand the depths of evil to which our community had plunged," he later wrote in a letter to me. "I thank God I went through this hell so I could see it for what it was."

On Saturday, March 16, 1968, in the first of the four trials in the Dahmer murder, a jury in Forrest County convicted

Sam Bowers's number-two man, Cecil Sessum, for his role in the killing. In his closing statement, prosecutor Jim Finch had urged the all-white jurors to search their hearts and remove racial prejudice in considering the case. He reminded them of the consequential fact that the "state of Mississippi" was bringing Sessum to justice—not the federal government up in Washington, D.C., as was the case with the previous trial for the murders of Chaney, Goodman, and Schwerner. This must not be forgotten, he said, the obvious implication being that Mississippi could take care of its business after all.

Finch had pointed directly to each juror and asked, "Do you believe any person or group has the right to violate the law of Mississippi just because of their race?"[9] He asked the jurors if they were willing to concede their towns to anarchy and violence. Finch was speaking not only of the prevailing reign of terror but also, more specifically, of Sessum's plump wife Mary, who had been apprehended on the morning of March 13 entering the courtroom with a loaded .38. Cecil Sessum's conviction was a big victory for the forces of justice in Jones and Forrest counties. Not only had a local jury convicted a white man for killing a Negro, but the presiding judge, a Mississippian named Stanton Hall, who whittled on a piece of cedar throughout the trial, sentenced Sessum, a tenth-grade dropout, to life in prison.

Sam Bowers, on the other hand, would be a tougher nut to crack. At his trial, which began a few weeks later, Bowers sat quietly in his courtroom chair, dressed in his Sunday-go-to-meeting best, his sandy-blond hair arranged in a sweeping shock. To be sure, the prosecutors were not lacking in incriminating evidence against him. The one-legged barber of Seminary, Mississippi, T. Weber Rogers, remembered Bowers's saying at a Klan meeting, "Something has to be done about that damn nigger down south." Vernon Dahmer was named as the Negro in question, Rogers said. He stated that Bowers ordered a dry run on the Dahmer property in the Kelly Settlement.

Klansman-turned-informant Billy Roy Pitts, who had worked at a furniture and upholstery shop in Laurel, showed an even keener eye for detail. Since his 1967 affidavit recounting the Dahmer murder, Billy Roy Pitts had emerged as the key witness against the Klan, although he had yet to make an appearance in the courtroom—and his identity had been protected until now. His much-anticipated entrance in the Forrest County courtroom—escorted by two sheriff's deputies—generated much excitement among onlookers and newspapermen. The *Laurel Leader-Call* reported: "The State is painfully aware of the fact [that] a bullet through the head or heart of its prized package could change in an instant the complexion of the first of a series of trials scheduled here in connection with [the] nationally publicized Vernon Dahmer case. The roosting place of the key witness between court appearances has remained as closely guarded as the man himself. Every precaution is being taken to discourage potential sharpshooters and snipers."[10]

After taking the oath, Pitts told the court he remembered that the meeting Rogers mentioned had been held on December 12, 1965, in a hay barn east of town. Bowers had appeared calm that night and in good spirits, leading the men in prayer, reciting the "kreeds," speaking in a steady voice. But as the meeting went on, and as he reviewed the Klan projects, he got angrier and angrier. By the end, he was screaming at the men and demanding that all overdue projects be taken care of immediately—especially the "job down south" in the Kelly Settlement.

But Bowers had prepared himself with a shrewd defense, mounted by the flamboyant attorney and socialite Lawrence Arrington. Arrington went after Pitts's credibility as a witness, telling the court of the former Klansman's sexual adventures at the Alamo Plaza Courts Motel in Jackson (carried out under the protective eyes of several U.S. marshals). He complimented Pitts on his sun-tanned skin, and probed him with a satirist's wit.

"So you've become the maharajah of the Alamo?"

"The what?" Pitts asked.

"The maharajah of the Alamo," Arrington repeated.

"You mean in Texas?" Pitts asked further.

"I mean in Jackson, Mississippi," said Arrington.

"No sir. I don't believe so."

Photos were produced of the big-chinned Pitts and a bikini-clad woman swimming in the motel pool. In one photo, a deputy marshal was seen splashing merrily in the shallow end. When Arrington asked Pitts where the federal guard had stored his guns when he went swimming, the state objected, and no answer was given.

Arrington brilliantly played to both sides of the aisle, manipulating public sentiment with a theatrical performance that left the courtroom agiggle. In a baritone as thick as sorghum, Arrington magnanimously reprimanded the Klan's violence while he extolled the virtues of fair trial in the same breath.

And a fair trial in this case meant coming to terms with the truth about Billy Roy Pitts.

"Billy Roy Pitts has been a liar ever since he entered the world," exclaimed a witness for the defense, Herman Jackson.

Pitts was a cad and a con. The jury had best entertain no illusions about him, confirmed Arrington. Pitts was so deep in the pockets of federal marshals it would take ten men to dig him out. He would say he was from Mars if they told him to.

But there was something more. Defense attorney Arrington welcomed to the courtroom Dr. Edwin Cole, the medical director of the South Mississippi State Hospital in Laurel. Dr. Cole told the jury that back in 1963 he'd treated the state's number-one witness for a condition known as "aeromegaly." "Pituitary giantism," he explained. Dr. Cole had been intrigued by the shape of Pitts's skull during a routine physical, in particular the "massively enlarged jaw which has increased progressively in size and interfered with the alignment of his teeth." The defense thanked the physician and surmised, without explanation, that no further evidence was needed to establish the fact of Pitts's mental incompetence. The *Laurel-Leader Call* noted, "But the doctor said there was no indication five years ago that Pitts was not mentally alert."[11]

Arrington claimed too that the only reason the trial was being held was that President Lyndon Johnson needed a conviction to bolster his popularity in the upcoming elections. "If there's no conviction, you may see that little man from Alabama up there running the show." He was talking about George Wallace, everyone knew, currently on the campaign trail for president as the third-party populist—though it was not at all clear why Arrington thought Wallace would pick up votes from people who wanted harsher prosecution of white-on-black violence.

Other witnesses were produced to convince the jury of the Imperial Wizard's decency. Bowers was a gentleman and a patriot, fair-minded to all. The witnesses paraded through the Hattiesburg courtroom included a former Klan sidekick from a shared business venture; a carpenter who moonlighted for the Americans for the Preservation of the White Race; Bowers's longtime roommate and confirmed bachelor from southern California, Robert Larson; and members of the Hillcrest Baptist Church where Bowers taught Sunday School. Sam Bowers was a fine Christian who never said an unkind word about black people. Even the Klan-hating County Attorney Charles Pickering was summoned for the defense. Pickering was asked three questions.

> **Arrington**: Do you know of Sam Bowers's reputation in the community?
> **Pickering**: Yes.
> **Arrington**: Is it good or bad?
> **Pickering**: It's bad.
> **Arrington**: Do you know that Sam Bowers teaches Sunday School?
> **Pickering**: Yes.
> **Arrington**: Thank you. That will be all.

Although being tried in south Mississippi in 1968 for killing black people might get a person caught in some annoying legal snares, any doubt about Bowers's involvement in Sunday School was serious business. (Still, Pickering's testimony earned him the respect of the Dahmer family, who wrote a letter of support when he was nominated by George Bush for the federal judiciary of south Mississippi.)

In an attempt to salvage the state's key witness, prosecutor Jim Finch conceded to the defense that Billy Roy Pitts was no-count. But trashy as Pitts was, his description of the Dahmer murder rang true. No deal had been struck to protect Pitts from imprisonment. Maybe he'd been given a few weeks R&R on the federal government's tab—that and a diet of sirloins at the Sun 'n' Sand Café. But no promises had been made to avoid prosecution or prison.

"You know where you're going when you get out of federal custody, don't you?" Finch asked his key witness, to add muscle to the point.

"Yes sir."

"And that's to Parchman prison?"

"Yes sir."

"And you know the Klan's rule for handling anyone who gives the kind of testimony you've given here?"

"Yes I do," Pitts said.

"What is the penalty?"

"Death," he answered, "clapping his lips and blowing out his cheeks," observed the *Leader-Call*.[12]

But death would be a nobler fate than cowardice, added a pleased Pitts. "I couldn't go along with the things being planned in Jones County—the killing and murdering and things."

On May 18, 1968, after twenty-two hours of jury deliberations, forty-four-year-old Imperial Wizard Sam Bowers was freed on a mistrial, even as allegations of jury tampering flew around the spring air like gnats. Eleven members of the all-white jury pushed for conviction, but one man favored acquittal. Bowers hugged the members of his legal team, smiled for the cameras, and got in his car and drove back to Laurel.

I don't want to suggest that my father's despair that spring was only about race, or about Marcus Cooley and Clifford Wilson, or about the trials of the White Knights of the Ku Klux Klan—not to mention the phone calls from the *New York Times* and the *Washington Post* seeking a little local color from the Baptist preacher-boy. It was also about his parents. His mother, Liz, for instance, took her son's humiliation as evidence of his hopeless naïveté. She had warned him of dabbling in racial matters. She'd read him the Citizens' Council publications, all the familiar prognostications of a mulatto race—or at least sent them to him in the mail, since he'd get up and leave the room when she started reading. "There have been instances of churches admitting Negroes since our last newsletter." The greatest threat to Mississippi society was "the man of conscience," one Council document stated without irony. "There is a straight line from the communists to the colored groups to sermons on peace," she wrote in a note. "You have no idea what you're doing!" Yet when she saw photos of him in the Jackson newspaper rubbing up to the Klansman, she felt vindicated all the same. He was incapable of sound judgment, an innocent, a buffoon. Forget whose side he was on.

His father, Howard, said nothing of the Jaycees banquet or south Mississippi burning, which came as no surprise, since he hadn't said much of anything to his son in years. Still, he found other ways of rubbing his son's face in it. My father was preaching his first Homecoming Day service in Laurel in anticipation of record crowds. He had prevailed upon his parents—with the help of my mother's handwritten pleas—to come for the weekend. Liz agreed, and promised that Howard would too. And he did. But hearing his son preach was not part of the plan.

Waking before sunrise on Sunday, Howard packed his Cadillac Seville with an ice chest full of beer and drove two hours to the coast. He spent the day fishing with friends. When my father learned of Howard's whereabouts before taking the pulpit for the eleven o'clock service, he turned ashen and stuttered his way through the morning announcements.

Our world grew insufferable, though I suppose we could have gone on this way for a while: my father morose and distant; my mother scrupulous and edgy, compensating too much for her husband's deracination; me bouncing like a marble on a string between them. One afternoon while I was in the den working on my coin collection, I heard my father's voice coming from my parent's bedroom. The door had been closed earlier when Mother and I returned from school. Dad was sleeping, I had figured. But now I could see inside. Mother was sitting on the bed next to him, and he was waving his hands in the air, saying in a sad voice, "Nobody understands, nobody. I just need someone to protect me. I just need a little help." Mother closed the door quickly when she saw me and stepped into the hall. She whispered that Dad was "delirious." If she'd had more time to think about it, I bet she would have used a different word. But "delirious" is what she said. My father didn't feel well, had come home from work early, and was delirious. She said Dr. Ledbetter was coming over soon with one of the B-12 shots he'd been giving my father a lot of lately, which always seemed to pick him up when he was feeling "draggy." In the meantime, I shouldn't bother him, she said. But a half hour later, with Dr. Ledbetter nowhere in sight, I saw my father walk into the weight room, wearing his cutoff jersey and his red sweatpants, ready for a workout. I kept my distance, riding my bike in figure eights in the cul-de-sac by our house.

Something had to give, or else the plain dread of life might have turned toward permanence, toward some never-ending way of being dead and flat. And something did.

"God hath chosen the foolish things of the world to confound the wise," the good apostle once said. He was speaking of redemption's comedy, on account of the one who repelled death's sting and defied the cosmic odds. He was speaking of the hilarity of grace, the way it sometimes hits you in the gut like a punch line. But God, if I may say so myself, outdid himself here.

12

Swimming Pools, Movie Stars, and Jesus Freaks

I was in the garage helping my father with his workout when Tommy Lester showed up. Tommy wore a skin-tight muscle shirt, stood six feet six, and was skinny as a rail. He had grown up in the cream-brick rancher across the street and attended the First Baptist Church until he left home for college. When he graduated from Ole Miss as a premed major, he told his friends in the Baptist Student Union that he was moving to Hollywood to make it in show business. When they called him crazy and said he didn't know the first thing about acting, he told them he'd done some things in Laurel before coming to college, played a ghost in a Halloween skit and a shoeshine boy in a Little Theater production. Besides, Hollywood needed an actor who was "tall and country and ugly." One night a few months later, Paul Henning, the producer and creator of "The Beverly Hillbillies," saw Tommy in a dinner theater performance of *Oklahoma*. He liked what he saw, and after an audition, signed him to the role of the nitwit Eb on the sitcom "Green Acres."

Tommy gave my father a whack on the shoulder that would have stunned a lesser man. When he saw me, he stretched out his arms in anticipation of a bear hug, and nearly threw me into the low ceiling with the force of his embrace. Then his eyes searched out mine, shifting to serious business. He squared off in front of me and slowly extended his flexed biceps (which quivered tightly in the air like a turkey beard). He told me to hit his arm, and I did. He howled laughing.

"Come on, man. You can do better than that. Hit me as hard you can," he said.

I hit him again.

"Let me show you a secret," Tommy said. "But keep it a secret, 'cause it could do some real damage if the word got out."

He clenched his fist in typical boxing fashion and punched me in the gut. I fell to the ground choking.

"Watch this, man. I'm gonna make a different kind of fist." He squeezed his fist so the base of the hand would strike first.

"How old are you?" he asked.

"Twelve," I said.

"Well then you're old enough to appreciate what I'm going to show you." And this time he punched me in the arm without warning. I slammed into the side of the garage.

"You feel the difference?" he asked.

I nodded, grimacing in pain.

"It's a Japanese technique, and you'll never have to worry about breaking your hand the way you used to."

"That's great," I said.

Tommy insisted on showing us his new weight-lifting routine involving dumbbells and padded bench. Just your basic bench press, but Dad and I weren't saying anything. Replacing the ten-pound weights with fifteen-pound slabs, he moved himself into a sitting position at the end of the bench. He slid his body under the bar and tested it to his liking. After marking equal distance from the two ends with his eyes, he fastened tightly onto the grips with his hands, inhaled and exhaled deeply, steadied his arm and back, steadied his face in a manner perpendicular to the bar, and lifted straightaway. With the weight airborne, things went awry: The bar wobbled like a dove winged by birdshot, and worse (since he'd forgotten to secure the lock-clamp), when his right arm pushed ahead of the left, swaying back and forth like a gospel singer, the left-side weights unloosed themselves and cascaded to the concrete floor, and then all the weights on his right side propelled the bar and his body and finally the bench itself into a heap of iron and flesh.

"I'm gonna be in Laurel only a few more days," he said upon resurfacing. "But before I go, Bob, I want an answer. Will you come out west in June and give us all a big dose of good ole' gospel preaching?"

On his feet and smiling, Tommy explained how the Spirit was moving over Hollywood and Los Angeles and the whole of southern California. "It's outta sight, man. You've gotta see it yourself. The scene's on fire."

He promised he'd set up some really cool speaking opportunities and rap sessions with youth leaders in the L.A. area along with a once-in-a-lifetime gig in the Sierra Nevadas at a retreat of the Haight-Ashbury Agape Fellowship. Tommy said he knew all the on-fire Christians in California and that the Haight scene was "groovy, man." You'd never know it was run by Southern Baptists, he joked. Tommy said he'd shared his testimony at one of their meetings and it was a great experience. Several kids had given their lives to Christ, although he had to admit they were a strange bunch of people and he really felt his own gifts were better served in the Hollywood vicinity. Tommy also said he'd show us Universal Studios and the houses of the celebrities and Disneyland. We would go yachting with his girlfriend, whose father owned a bunch of Bob's Big Boy restaurants. We'd have a blast.

"You pray about it now. I'll be back over tomorrow afternoon. You really can't say no to this, can you, man?"

We prayed about it that night at dinnertime, even though we had each in our own way already sensed God's will in favor of the trip. "Going to California might be the best thing for us," my father said. "It's an unbelievable mission field out there." A midsummer revival in Shreveport would have to be rescheduled—which would not go over well since it was almost May. He'd probably be giving up the opportunity of a repeat invitation. But my father said he didn't mind. "Right now the thought of Shreveport just makes my heart sink," he said. "No, I think I'll call Tommy and say yes." Mother nodded her head solemnly in agreement. I agreed, too, even though I was thinking more of movie stars and sunny beaches and the promise of a visit with the fab pig Arnold Ziffel of "Green Acres" fame.

We prepared for the journey each in our own way. My father had his secretary order some back issues of *Village Voice*, so he could familiarize himself with the mindset of the counter-culture, offer a sympathetic word to the hippies about Cage and Warhol and Huxley. He also wrote the First Baptist congregation and shared with them the burdens of his heart. "I have never in all my ministry felt such a real need for somebody to lift me to God in daily prayer. The pressure of being keenly prepared, the realization that so many are now depending on me to come through, and the overwhelming fact that before me will be hundreds of lost souls, cause me to call on you dear people to pray."[1] My mother studied her Bible, as she always did daily, but now scribbling into the margins of her Philips version edifying words for the moment at hand. Alongside the story of Amos (the unlikely tender of sycamore trees God called from the backwaters to speak judgment on the nation), she wrote, "Raise up Bob, O Lord, to proclaim your precious and Holy Word." I used my allowance to buy some reading materials for the trip west: the latest *Mad* magazines on sale at the Busy Bee and a book of jokes involving a little boy with a crew cut named Marvin.

One morning a few weeks after school ended, we boarded a DC-8 in Atlanta and flew across the southern expanse of America to begin our stay on the West Coast. We arrived in Los Angeles in early afternoon. Since the "Green Acres" cast was in the studio filming for the fall season, Tommy's girlfriend picked us up and drove us to her home in Pacific Palisades. The front door of the guest cottage opened onto a tropical garden and a swimming pool surrounded by palm trees. The next few days were long, languorous, perfect. When my father went off to breakfast one morning with some home missionaries in the area—men and women working for the Southern Baptist Mission Board to evangelize unsaved territories on the domestic front—I stayed at the guest cottage with my mother and swam in the pool. I lounged on a cushioned divan reading *Mad* magazines. I ate mountains of boiled shrimp and melon and homemade ice cream. One day we all went sailing on Balboa Bay, and I steered the Big Boy yacht into ocean waters. One day we saw Bob Gibson throw a one-hitter for the St. Louis Cardinals at Dodger Stadium. In the evenings—or if my father preached, after the service—we'd hang out with Tommy's church friends, eat pizza or hamburgers, go swimming after supper. It seemed as if everyone had a pool in Los Angeles.

As promised, I also visited Universal Studios. You'd have thought I was their long-lost Mississippi cousin, the way the folks from Hooterville welcomed me to the set. There were Haney and Kimball, Ziffel and Drucker (whose general store also served "Petticoat Junction"), the house painter, Ralf Monroe, and Alf, his androgynous partner, and Arnold the pig. Tommy whispered in my ear (since it was common knowledge that Christians needed to be as wise as serpents in winning the pagans) that Mr. Haney had recently surrendered his life to Christ, and I whispered back, "praise the Lord." I didn't let on to the friendly walleyed salesman that I knew whose side he was on, but I felt my heart warm toward my new brother in the Spirit.

Tommy led me into the large aluminum building that housed Paul Henning Productions, then through a series of steel fire doors into a darkened room. He told me to stand still while he turned on the lights. A vast interior space the size of an airplane hangar appeared before my eyes, revealing the house of Jed Clampett and kin. The view from the cement pond. We entered Granny's kitchen—where vittles like possum and sweet potatoes and Jethro's favorite cooter-pie simmered night and day—and walked into the dining room, where we encountered a thicket of electrical wires, cameras, sound equipment, and wall-sized murals of the Clampett compound and the world outside—the stately Drysdale residence, the green hills and meadows of Beverly Hills in the distance. Beyond, we gathered in the Clampetts' foyer, atop the marble floor (a glossy linoleum in fact), surrounded by the winding staircase, the grandfather clock, the tapestries and paintings. We pressed forward, through the front door, into the driveway, where the famous jalopy rested in Appalachian splendor.

"Hop in," Tommy instructed.

I took Granny's seat and armed myself with her shotgun, which rested on the floorboard, and Tommy got behind the wheel. We drove back and forth along the semicircular driveway, singing triumphantly,

Let me tell you an ole story 'bout a man named Jed
Poor mountaineer barely kept his family fed
But then one day he was shooting up some food
And up through the ground come-a bubbling crude,
Oil, that is, black gold, Texas tea,

until I was laughing so hard my sides hurt.

We met my parents for lunch at the studio restaurant. Several times during the meal, tourists approached the table asking for Eb's autograph and sometimes my father's. The tanned, muscular man in the polo shirt must be somebody famous, too. Tommy introduced us to other celebrities dining in the restaurant: Jack Webb (chain-smoking but polite), Tiny Tim ("a real searcher", Tommy said, "keep him in your prayers"), and Dean Jones (soon to become famous in *Love Bug*). When Jones was introduced to my mother, he took her hand and kissed it with a dramatic finish, and launched her lifelong fascination with a man she considers one of the great actors in movie history.

Early the next morning we set out for the retreat in northern California. My father was all business. He had opened up on the front seat a map of the state with the day's destination marked in red felt-tip pen as well as the *Los Angeles Times* weather report. He had also purchased a pharmacy bag of travel provisions: vitamins, a bottle of Pepto-Bismol, Listerine, some Ayds chocolate chews, a suppository, throat lozenges, a *Street and Smith's College Football Annual*, and a vial of antibiotics in case we needed them. He had personally checked the engine of the rental car—tapped his fingers against a hose running from a pipe, pulled at the air filter cover to make sure it was screwed on tight. He knew nothing about automobiles. My mother was reading her Bible, and reminded my father to pray for the trip just as he was about to put the car in gear. So he prayed for the usual things: for traveling mercies upon us. That Christ would be edified in all our words and actions. But when he turned his thoughts to the upcoming week, his voice trembled softly as he said, "Oh God, make us instruments of your will in reaching the lost youth of America."

We drove up Interstate 99 toward San Francisco and then west along State Highway 108 into the Stanislaus National Forest. The air was cooler in the mountains, the sky blue and clear, and the mood lightened. By the time we arrived at the camp in Jennes Park after lunch, my father was telling funny stories about himself. Like the one about scoring the winning basket for the opposing team in high school, or the three-hundred-pound man who slipped during a baptismal service and sent waves of water crashing over the protective glass into the choir.

The colorful hand-painted Spiritbuses from the Haight-Ashbury Fellowship had already arrived, bringing several hundred college and high school students to the mountain retreat. I had seen hippies of the Southern variety lounging around Jackson Square in New Orleans, and I'd heard many a cautionary word about the devilish counterculture brewing in the Bay Area. But this was the real thing, baby. The epicenter of world hippiedom, temporarily relocated two hundred miles east.

We entered a strange world, beginning with the youth leader who greeted us outside the cafeteria with his index finger pointed in the "one-way Jesus" sign. The man—whom we were introduced to as Kent—looked a lot like the Savior himself, the Warner Sallman version at least, long brown hair falling to shoulders, the eyes gently expectant, the beard, and the poncho. No doubt if he had shown up in Laurel looking like this, someone would have called Sheriff Merle and had him brought in for questioning. But Kent was an evangelist under the employment of the Southern Baptist Convention and was turning acidheads on to Jesus and baptizing them in record numbers. The suits who ran the Home Mission Board in Nashville didn't care much for longhairs—or evangelistic innovation in general—but they loved the stats Kent was putting up. He welcomed us with open arms and rapid-fire "praise Jesuses," "right ons," and "hallelujahs." He offered me a soul-slap, raised up his hand, palm side down—"give me some skin, brother," and I stuck out my hand and smiled.

Our home for the week was a forest-green cabin beside a stream, equipped with hot plate and fridge in the kitchen, woodstove, and toilet. If we wanted a bath, we could use the mountain waters. There was a double bed in the main room next to the woodstove, and a single roll-out tucked into a nook alongside the kitchen. I told my parents there was no way I was going to sleep back there, and rolled the bed into the main room next to theirs.

The retreat began in the late afternoon. A large canvas tent was pitched in a recently mowed field to serve as the common meeting place. The field was surrounded by meadows and the snowcapped mountains in the distance. The students slept in cabins built on the periphery, with a cafeteria, recreation building, tennis courts, and softball diamond a short walk away.

Our days had little structure apart from the evening worship service. The daily events happened spontaneously, we were told, according to the moving of the Spirit. We were "resisting the sterility of organized religion," Kent explained. Throughout the week, there were pray-ins, sing-ins, be-ins, hug-ins, and rap sessions. Sometimes staffers and students sat alone in fields, picking wildflowers and leaves of grass, or staring into the starry skies at night, encouraged "to spend a little personal time with God."

The girls flocked to my mother, made her an honorary hippie, and told her the details of their psychedelic and erotic escapades, and she listened patiently and nonjudgmentally as usual. A girl named Daisy gave her a Guatemalan blouse and a headband of flowers. Daisy had a black boyfriend and had taken LSD seventeen times, my mother learned. And she'd found God during one recent hallucination—the most beautiful experience of her life, serene, full of peace, like a meadow of flowers. Daisy said that she'd decided to come to the retreat when she saw the fliers in a coffee shop and fell in love with the photograph of the campgrounds. My mother had never heard a testimony quite like hers, but she didn't immediately refuse Daisy's claims. She spoke of faith as a pilgrimage, a "providential tapestry" woven together in Christ, and surmised that even an epiphany as strange as Daisy's might still "be used by God to accomplish his purposes." My mother was working hard "to relate," "to make faith relevant," as Kent had asked of my parents, but the simple message of purity and peril did not seem to be getting through, and I think my mother knew it.

My father couldn't find anyone who shared an interest in Southeastern Conference football, but he made his mark just the same. He stopped shaving for the week, initially due to lack of hot water. At home, he was a two-a-day man, but in California, he let it go for good. He liked the way the beard linked him to the prevailing spirit of dissent and how it was appreciated by all, including my mother. I told him if he didn't shave it by the time he got home, he'd get fired, and he looked me straight in the eye and laughed. He'd also read enough about Camus and Sartre in seminary to keep up with most Berkeley dropouts. He attracted a group of guys who wore army fatigues and smoked cigarettes, and they huddled together and talked about "dialectic" and "resistance" and "the pursuit of an alternative consciousness." Still, when I found my father leading a rap session one afternoon on the music of the Rolling Stones ("meeting the kids where they're at," he explained later), pausing occasionally to play a cut from "Their Satanic Majesties Request," I thought I was hallucinating.

My father had always seemed so far removed from things like pop music and offbeat ideas and from just hanging out and shooting the bull. And it always seemed he had to be right—like when he preached a sermon, you couldn't disagree with him about anything without making him angry or nervous. But the hippies were disagreeing with him, sometimes shaking their heads in frustration, like when he told them that "we'll all be a thousand light-years from home until we open our hearts to God," or "Give Mick Jagger credit for admitting that he doesn't know wrong from right, because it takes a heart cleansed by the blood of Jesus to wash our consciences clean." When the hippies objected that Jesus was just a crutch or a myth, or maybe a prophet but not God, he came right back. "If we don't search for truth with a capital T, we're all going to end up like Brian Jones." Not a bad call, since the Stones' guitarist wouldn't be dead for a year. (My father was thinking of the recent nine-month prison sentence for drug charges.) The man was on a roll.

Rock music soared from the loudspeakers nailed into telephone poles around the central field. At Lake Forest Ranch, the youth camp in northern Mississippi and site of most of my father's prior guest appearances, the only music you'd hear was Tennessee Ernie Ford—and that only to wake us up in the morning. But in California, a hippie named Mark invited me to the meadow where his friends stood in anticipation and pointed to the speakers, beckoning silence with his finger. As a Hammond organ laid down a hypnotic beat, followed by guitars, drums, and bass, Mark and I were joined by more campers coming from other points of the fields, from the cabins, the cafeteria, the footpaths along the hillside. We were soon dancing to the drowsy rhythms of "In-a-Gadda-da-Vita" and didn't stop until the last bar of the seventeen-minute song had come to an end.

Kent insisted we also listen to some songs by a friend of his named Larry Norman. Norman was a puckish songwriter with long blond hair and an acned face. He would be known to many in the Bay Area for his columns in *Right On!*—the

Berkeley free paper published by the World Liberation Front, a Christian alternative for disillusioned members of the secular Left (as the WLF claimed). By the end of the 1960s, Norman would appear regularly as the star attraction in the "Jesus-rock" fests that were created to rival Woodstock and the Isle of Wight, the most influential songwriter of the Jesus movement. But for now, he was still just hanging out with his younger sister and her friends at Richard's Christian Halfway House, or at the Living Room, or at any of the other Jesus-freak coffee shops and hostels in the Bay Area. He was working with a rock band called People, writing songs and recording them in his basement, not quite sure where he was going to end up— he hadn't completely given up drugs—but yet certain he wanted to be called a Jesus freak. Norman believed that in the teachings of Christ, he had found the missing piece of the counterculture, the hidden source of its dreams and hopes, God made rebel flesh, divinity at the margins. He was writing pamphlets criticizing the pop music industry—stars like Clapton, Jagger, and Paige who exploited black musical genius, ripping off musical form at the expense of religious depth. He was also scolding the mainline evangelical church for its complicity in racism, ecological decay, Vietnam, and all-around bourgeois smugness. Norman combined a quirky evangelical piety with radical politics and unleashed his sneering anger on old-time believers like some born-again Sid Vicious, offending both left and right along the way.

> *I was born and raised an orphan*
> *In a land that once was free*
> *In a land that poured its love out on the moon.*

And I grew up in the shadows
Of your silos filled with grain,
But you never helped to fill my empty spoon.

You killed a black man at midnight
Just for talking to your daughter,
Then you made his wife your mistress
And you leave her without water.
And the sheet you wear upon your face
Is the sheet your children sleep on
And at every meal you say a prayer
You don't believe but still you keep on.

And your money says "In God We Trust"
But it's against the law to pray in school
You say we beat the Russians to the moon
And I say you starved your children to do it.
You say all men are equal, all men are brothers
Then why are the rich more equal than others
Don't ask me for the answers, I've only got one,
That a man leaves his darkness when he follows the Son.

This was a long way from "Rock of ages cleft for me/let me hide myself in thee." Mark and his friends dug it, and so did I.

A Mexican family named Garcia lived in one of the staff houses on the hillside behind the cafeteria. Jorge, the father, was an ordained Baptist minister who'd pastored a biracial church in Pasadena before taking a job at the camp. One evening we ate a meal together on card tables at their home, the Garcias and their five children, Kent and his wife, and my family. Jorge grilled chickens and served them with a platter of tortillas and enchiladas. We drank fruit punch from tall plastic cups. I listened as the family sang the blessing in Spanish.

After supper, the children and I played baseball in a nearby field. I told the Garcia kids I liked their mom's cooking. I usually didn't like Mexican food. I'd eaten it once in a TV dinner and gotten a stomachache. But I liked eating with them. The chicken reminded me of Dixie League barbecues, so tender it just fell off the bone. I told them they should come visit me in Mississippi. We could go eat chicken at the baseball park. We could play on the same team, too.

One of the older kids laughed out loud.

"You think we could go to a baseball game with you?" he asked.

"Sure," I replied, and laughed with him. "There's a great swimming hole I know up at Walkaway Springs, and they've got a high dive and the coldest water you've ever felt."

"We're Mexicans, haven't you noticed?" he said.

"I know that. We could grill chickens up there. They have some barbecue pits you can use."

"Do you know what that means? We're niggers!" he said before I could answer.

"No you're not," I said, taken aback by his words.

"The big fat sheriff would lock us up in jail. He'd beat us with his billy club. He'd chain us to a tree and make a bonfire."

"No he wouldn't," I said. "That's not right. Don't say that."

His words saddened me. I felt confused and afraid. But the children were smiling, waiting for more.

"The KKK would stand around the bonfire in the white sheets and sing the KKK songs. 'We've caught us some niggers. We're grilling us some niggers. The Mexican kind. A little bit spicy.'"

The other Garcias were laughing now.

"Stop it," I said. "I don't know what you're talking about. You shouldn't say that."

"Well, you will soon enough," the brother said. And with that said, he held up a baseball and tossed it softly toward me. I reached out and caught it in my glove.

When the sun had set on the field and forest, we walked up the hillside back to the house. The brother put his hand around my shoulder and said, "I'm sorry I scared you a little back there. I've just never seen a Mississippi boy before. You're going to be okay, aren't you?"

"Yeah," I said. "I'll be okay."

"Just don't forget about us Garcias," he said.

"I won't," I said, and we raced the distance to the porch.

Inside the house, Jorge was playing the guitar. His wife stood next to him shaking a tambourine. In the middle of the living room, my mother was dancing with my father. I'd never seen her dance before. Dancing was the devil's business—Baptists didn't make love standing up, the joke went, because it might lead to dancing—and here was my mother, red-faced, nearly ecstatic, swinging between my father and Kent in syncopated rhythm. I stood at the doorway and watched. It was no joking matter. I had always abstained from dancing at school parties. Honoring my body as the "Temple of the Holy Spirit" was right up there at the top of the list of my Man of God Essentials. I would stand near the snack table with a few other pure souls and look disdainfully on the whole wretched scene before me. When my grandmother Lilly told me one day that my mother had danced in high school, I confronted her with the shocking discovery, nearly reducing her to tears when she realized the full extent of my feelings—anger, betrayal, disappointment. She'd told me she was sorry and tried to persuade me that her social dancing preceded her commitment to Christ—but I didn't believe her for a second, which only fueled my anger. But that was then. Now, in California, my mother wasn't apologizing for anything. She was winking her eye at me instead, just before spinning around into my father's arms and shouting "Olé!" "Olé, my foot!" It was as if she'd been doing this kind of thing for years, and I blushed with embarrassment at the sight.

The last afternoon my father and I spent relaxing on the banks of the mountain stream that ran beneath our cabin. The air was dry, and the sunlight poured through the fir trees in clean lines on the surface of the water.

I had taken off my T-shirt, letting the sunshine warm my skin. We were talking about the week that was nearly over. My father had asked my impressions about the friends I had made, the new adventures, and the new ideas. He asked about the areas of my life that had been touched or convicted or changed. How had I grown in the Lord?

I told him I really wanted to get the Larry Norman album when it came out.

"I like him a lot," I said, "We should think about getting him to Laurel. I bet the kids in the church would like him, too.

I bet he could fire everybody up." I liked having my father next to me on the smooth ground.

"Let's pray about that," he said, looking at me with a smile.

"Where can you get Larry Norman albums in Mississippi?" I asked, blowing a cluster of dandelions into a soft breeze.

"Now that's a good question," he said. "I guess Mrs. Moates at the Baptist Book Store could order them."

"Or we could get Kent to send us some in the mail," he added after a pause.

"You think I could start a rock band in Laurel, a Christian rock band? We could play at "Saturdays in the Park" and at youth revivals. Johnny Helveston could play bass. And Joey could play drums. I know his momma would like that. She'd be glad to hear him play something besides "Wipeout."

"What instrument would you play?" my father asked.

"I could sing, or play the guitar like Brother Garcia, something like that."

"That's an interesting idea. Let's pray about that, too." He closed his eyes and leaned back in the grass. His body was still.

"Dad, I've been thinking about Mississippi, you know, going home, what it's going to be like. I kind of like it out here. Maybe we could come back sometime and stay longer."

"I've been thinking about Mississippi, too," he said. "Feels like a long way away, doesn't it?"

"Yeah. I don't really miss it." I was surprised by my boldness.

"You know what, son? I can't believe I'm saying this, but I don't miss it either."

He started laughing, and I laughed too.

"Hey, Brother Bob. Up here!" The voice came from the hillside above us. The hippie Mark and his girlfriend waved from the hiking trail across the stream.

We waved back and smiled.

"You know what I'm doing, preacher?" Mark shouted.

"Looks like you're taking a hike," my father said.

"Guess again. What do you think I'm doing?"

My father threw up his hands.

"You're communing with nature," he said.

"I'm walking the Jesus path!" Mark shouted.

With his long curly hair tied back in a red bandanna, you could see his face light up in a smile.

When my father tried to answer, his voice broke. He offered Mark a simple "one-way" sign in response, and the hikers disappeared over the hill.

My father turned to me, started to speak, then stopped himself. After a moment of silence, he said, "I love you, son."

"Me, too," I said, reaching forward and plunging my hand into the cold stream, splashing water across his bearded face.

We packed up the rental car the next morning, and as we were headed down the dirt road to the main highway for the drive to the San Francisco airport, I watched the tall trees blur into a blue-green streak across the bright sky. I told my parents I hoped this hadn't all been a dream. But by the silence that descended and remained with us for long stretches of time on the trip home, I could tell that none of us was sure.

Still, none of us would ever be the same. That was for sure. The notion that God could use hippies, freaks, and radicals "to accomplish his purposes" seemed as unexpected to my parents as it did to me. We never thought you might hear the voice of God talking among outsiders and outcasts. More than once during the week, my father had recalled his encounter with Marcus Cooley and decided it *was* high time he started listening. My mother wrote in her Bible that she'd learned to trust God in "fresh and exciting ways," to "turn over her fears to the Almighty Father, our refuge from danger." I figured that if God could use Mark and Daisy, he could use anybody, or anything. "You've got to get out of your safe haven and make your witness count, you gotta make it street level," Mark had told me as were saying our farewells. I wasn't sure exactly what he meant. But the words came together somehow in my mind in the form of a big wide-open space. And it was as if God suddenly filled that space, and the thought seared its way into irrevocable memory and imagination, so that every time thereafter when I thought of God, I thought of great expanses of light and freedom, and I thought of California.

13

Are We in the Promised Land Yet?

Some historians of American religion would later describe the Jesus movement as the first stirrings of the dreaded Christian right, a socially conservative reaction to the breakdown of traditional morality during the student revolutions.[1] In fact, it's true that by the end of the 1970s, the movement's focus had shifted from the margins to the mainline; longhaired Jesus freaks were replaced by telegenic preachers in Brooks Brothers suits and political crusaders running PACs and lobbies. The Christian counterculture had given way to family values; cultural engagement to culture wars; Larry Norman to Amy Grant.

But in Laurel, Mississippi, in the fall of 1968, the Jesus movement, as it was transplanted onto the carpeted floors of First Baptist Church, offered us a wholly new outlook on our Southern home, and no one regarded it as conservative for a minute. Mark's picture appeared on the cover of *Newsweek* magazine in September. He'd kept his hair long, and his arms were outstretched in pentecostal ecstasy, as were those of the other converts gathered in a public park in San Francisco. My father, minus facial hair—"Mississippi humidity got the better of me on this one"—slipped the photo under his desk glass.

His sermons changed accordingly, not so much the style (though that changed too in the fashionable drift toward pop-cultural relevance) but the substance. The suffocating theology of the closed society, with its creepy platitudes on hell and holiness, had now to be pushed aside in one defiant spiritual stiff-arm (still my father's preferred vernacular), the new seized with abandon like a fullback breaking through the secondary into the end zone. He told us to listen to culture, to learn from it, to hear what it was saying about God and the human condition.

> Are we hearing the right questions of our day? You Christians, in a world of hate, war, racial strife, and suffering, do you have a message of life, love, and redemption—and is that message backed up by radical living? Because if the "church" is a stepping-stone for social, political, and economic ladder-climbers, a denominational merry-go-round, a hot-bed for developing the status-quo, a place where we talk about loving God and people

but a place which excludes any concept of God or person who does not fit into our mold, then maybe it should die, be buried in the graveyard of irrelevancy, and covered with the dirt of shame!

But wait a minute! What if "the church" is something more than a blood-pressure-raising organization, than having harmless meetings, talking about missions but scorning some people for whom Christ died?

Real religion is faith with its sleeves rolled up, out there where it's happening, on the fringes where Jesus lived. "Jesus was crucified at the crossroads, out near the garbage dump, between two thieves amidst profanity and blasphemy. That is what his death was all about, and that is what the church is all about." Jesus called people "to take up their cross, not their cushion," to venture out of their comfort zones and "to act boldly on their new freedom in Christ."

To his congregation of Citizens' Councilors and Jaycee enthusiasts, he praised the student dissidents, their courage and conviction. He contemplated rebellion as metaphor. Faith, like freedom, is "perpetual risk, an exhausting adventure." The students were right to call the church on its phoniness. "We *have* made religion an opiate," he said. Look at these beautiful young people linked in utopian dreams across the American continent. See them as men and women thirsting for God as a deer thirsts for water.

He purchased a full-page ad in the *Leader-Call*, a psychedelic montage of Holy Ghost fire, and arms raised in fields of praise, long hair whipping like fiery sparks, electric guitars punctuating the scene like lightning bolts. "Don't Knock It," the caption read. "Maybe you don't like rock and roll, but there's vibrancy to its beat that lets kids express themselves. Even if it isn't your kind of music, it's their kind of music. Perhaps the 'generation gap' may be narrowed slightly if you'll listen." Then came the thundering question, "Have you gone with your teenager to church lately?"

He peppered his sermons with citations of Russell and Orwell, Hemingway and Faulkner, Orwell and Eliot; secular parables of man's search for meaning. He bought synopses of the classics, the Durants' *History of Western Thought*, William Barrett's *Irrational Man*, Kierkegaard and Dostoyevsky, modern drama on tape. As for Camus, his favorite, the big-hearted humanist with the praying mother, Camus convicted. "What the world expects of Christians is that Christians should speak out, loud and clear . . . and should get away from abstraction and confront the blood-stained face history has taken on today," Camus said. Christians must "speak out clearly and pay up personally."

Larry Norman may not have been able to fit Mississippi on his itinerary, but the Pilgrim 20 Singers of the University of Kansas squeezed us in, along with various regional bands and folk combos singing the new Jesus rock. When a folk singer from Metarie, Louisiana, played a cover of "Blowin' in the Wind" with the chorus revised to "The answer, my friend, is Jesus Christ the Lord," the resulting lyrical distress seemed a small price to pay for reaching the lost youth of America. (My daydreams of a rock band would be realized only in the privacy of my bedroom, with the help of an RCA record player and a tennis racket for air guitar.) After the Sunday evening service, the sanctuary would be rearranged, the pulpit removed, along with the heavy ornamented chairs and offering table. Drums, mikes, and amps were put in their place. The students wore jeans and turtlenecks—the days of starched poplin gone at last. We got down evangelical style, swayed back and forth, held hands for "Kumbaya," "Pass It On," and "Get Together," sometimes danced in the aisles (minus the thrust and grind and the charismatic jitters).

Francis Schaeffer also came to town that fall. Schaeffer was the hip theologian of the evangelical subculture. Years earlier he had traded his pinstriped suits for a pair of knickers, grown a goatee, and assumed the exaggerated air of a tortured intellectual. He founded a Christian commune in the Swiss Alps and armed himself with a paragraph's worth of prose on nearly every major writer and artist in Western civilization. He authored many short but highly ambitious books, such as *The God Who Is There*, *Escape from Reason*, and *Pollution and the Death of Man*. Many featured dramatic flowcharts illustrating humanism's calamitous defeat of revelation and "propositional Truth." Schaeffer bemoaned nihilism, existentialism, liberalism, absurdism, dadaism. He told us we lived in a split-level universe, irrationality occupying the upper story, quashing reason and natural law into oblivion. "Modern theology has not helped us," he wrote flatly. "From Karl Barth on, it is an upper-story phenomenon. Faith is a totally upstairs leap. The difference with modern theology is that it is really no different from taking drugs. You may take drugs, you may try modern liberal theology. It makes no difference—both are trips, separated from reason."[2]

Schaeffer rendered steady judgment against the American church's intellectual malaise, warning us from his alpine perch that our bourgeois slumber would prove our undoing. We must read, think, study, analyze, debate. "The churches must take truth seriously."

My father had learned that Schaeffer was scheduled to speak at a youth convention in San Diego. So he telegrammed him in Huemoz, Switzerland, with the invitation to stop by Laurel on his way to the West Coast. He offered a thousand-dollar honorarium, the Gardiner suite at the Pinehurst Hotel, and whatever expenses Schaeffer needed to reroute the flight from Geneva through Atlanta.

So here was Francis Schaeffer in Laurel—if you can imagine it—at a special Thursday evening "apologetics seminar" in the Fellowship Hall, making the few dozen parishioners in attendance watch an Ingmar Bergman film, "Face to Face," and listen to a composition by John Cage. Schaeffer's eyes were swollen with tears when the lights came back on and the last dissorant bar of "Atlas Eclipticalisa" had come to a screeching halt. When a young lawyer in town giggled at the sight of a Jackson Pollack painting during the slide show, "Modern Art and Cosmic Alienation," Schaeffer lost his temper, accusing the poor fellow of showing just the kind of intellectual shabbiness that had destroyed classical Christianity. When he lectured, we scribbled in our notebooks "form and freedom," "autonomous reason," "existential despair," often scanning our neighbor's notes for help. Screaming about secularism was a familiar sound in my Christian milieu, but no one had ever urged us with such passion to engage the day, "to seize the

modern mind for God." He showed us a strange and perplexing world so much bigger than our own.

My father wrote Schaeffer a letter after his visit and asked,
"How can I talk to young people about purity when all of the
values we hold dear are being destroyed by immorality and a
loss of shame?" Schaeffer replied, "Without love, purity becomes hard, proud and legalistic," hoping to illuminate a
broader social space for Christian faith and practice.

With all the strange new energy buzzing through the
building, it was only a matter of time before "life deacons"
(elected for life) and the old-timers crashed the party. These
guardians of the Baptist tradition feared "a cultural takeover in
the shadows," as my father wrote in a letter to a pastor colleague. Church was just fine the way it had always been, they
insisted, with songs from the *Baptist Hymnal*, a robed choir, a
twenty-five-minute sermon followed by two verses of the invitational hymn "Just As I Am" and a prompt benediction. Bob
Marsh should take his new act over to St. John's Episcopal,
where the bearded priest had been wearing Nehru jackets to
civic gatherings and hosting chablis and cheese receptions in
his manse near the museum. (My father was content with
Barq's and boiled peanuts, but thanks anyway.) The old-timers
at First Baptist cautioned my father to put on the brakes. Electric guitars and drums don't belong in a Baptist church, much
less guest speakers dressing like the cast of "Laugh-In." But he
argued his case; this church needs "joy, life and a more spontaneous atmosphere," he wrote in a newsletter. "Don't discourage our young people from getting excited about what Christ
is doing in their lives, even if it makes you uncomfortable."

In an effort to bring both sides together, my father asked the members of the rock group Truth—who were booked for an upcoming Sunday evening slot—to sing the offertory hymn at the 11:00 a.m. service. He hoped this would give everyone a chance to know each other better, since the band leader had promised to play a song with broad appeal. My father had in mind something like an up-tempo "On Christ the Solid Rock I Stand," but instead he got a red-headed woman dressed in a black maxi singing "Ode to Billy Joe." Neither side appreciated Truth's little joke. Sam Pack, a chain-smoking octogenarian and influential deacon, cornered my father after church and gave him a piece of his mind. Pack told him he was personally responsible for "desecrating the House of the Lord." "Preacher, I knew something like this was gonna happen sooner or later," he said. "We're going to be the laughingstock of Mississippi Baptists."

So my parents began hosting the weekly Bible studies and youth events in our home. On Thursday afternoons, cases of RC Cola and Nehi grape soda arrived courtesy of Mac MacInish, a parishioner who owned the local bottling company. Jimmy Shoemaker supplied fresh-cut flowers at my mother's request, arranged in vases on the dining room table and scattered freely on the mantel or beneath the picture window on the front porch. The living room furniture was rearranged to clear a large space for the students, who preferred sitting on the floor.

After a quick supper—a few takeouts from the hot tamale stand on Ishee Street—the doorbell began ringing. In the first weeks, attendance was modest—twenty or thirty students huddling around my father with open Bibles—but by the middle of the fall the crowds were spilling out to the porch and into the kitchen and den. The front windows and doors were wide open, every lamp and fixture welcoming strangers in. Our house, which had once been sealed tight by fear and a homemade alarm system, now felt like our own little camp in the woods—8 Highland Woods to be exact. By the end of the fall, after a week when two hundred kids showed up at the house, the gatherings were moved to the Masonite Ballroom at the Pinehurst Hotel.

My father's hopes for an "on-fire" church were finally realized. A state Baptist newspaper writer described the scene:

> The young people enjoyed an all-youth picnic at Lake Shelby near Hattiesburg. . . . Junior Day was held at Daphne Park. . . . A "Think-in" was staged at the J. W. King home. . . . The J. W. Fagans hosted a "Beach-Out." . . . A junior high fellowship was held at Joe Roberts home. . . . Junior Day was enjoyed at the Laurel Skating Rink. . . . Thirty-two young people attended Ridgecrest Music Week. . . . High school fellowships were held at the W. O. Barnett and the Frank Warnock and the John Low homes. . . . A "Think-in" was held at Stafford Springs. . . . The Vesper Choir presented "Purpose," a musical, at the church and later to the Don't Mention Age Club at the YWCA and to the Laurel Kiwanis Club. The musical was dubbed "a singout sound of the sixties.". . . The young people were challenged to feel the exhilaration of each new day, to know the joy of freedom that was theirs by giving their lives to Christ, to be free to accept themselves—free to love, to share, to give, to feel the deep satisfaction of lives lived for others, and to be sure of their commitment to God.[3]

But it was not only the Jesus movement that was gaining momentum in the fall of 1968. All the usual Klan suspects in our neck of the woods were once again being hauled in by the carloads to a Forrest County courtroom.

When Sam Bowers had been freed on a mistrial back in the spring for the killing of Vernon Dahmer, James Finch, the district attorney trying the case, had promised the jury members after the verdict was read that he intended to stand tall against the Klan, and he expected them all to do the same. He refused to be intimidated. "They can bring all the wizards and lizards and thugs from Jones County down here, and I still won't back off," he resolved. Finch also promised to seek a new court date and to try the cases "until a verdict is reached—one way or the other," to try them "just as hard and just as long as the state of Mississippi knows how."[4]

For the fact was, in killing Vernon Dahmer, the Klan had gone too far. Vernon Dahmer was a local. He worked hard. He paid his bills. He owned a sawmill, a planer mill, a country store, and a 200-acre farm. He was a member of the Shady Grove Baptist Church along with his eight children and pretty wife, Ellie Jewel. He even served as the church's unpaid music director. He wasn't some militant hothead, forever jockeying for airtime. He looked out for his own, whites liked to say.[5] One white civic leader eulogized him as "a strong believer in America, Mississippi, Forrest County, his community, education, church, and family unity." The *Hattiesburg American* even issued a blistering editorial against the White Knights, calling on all Forrest County residents to help bring Bowers to justice. A handful of local whites pledged to rebuild the store and house. With the killing of Vernon Dahmer, public sentiment began to turn solidly against the Klan, as its henchmen would soon discover.

On July 19, 1968, W. T. Smith, another of Bowers's henchmen, was found guilty of first-degree murder and arson and was sentenced to life in prison by Judge Stanton Hall—the second life term given in the Dahmer murder. Smith had his character witnesses too, including Joe "Hamburger" Harrison, constable of Beat 1 of Jones County, but Hamburger's testimony flopped when the jury learned he had once joined the Klan only to quit after hearing about the ten-dollar dues. Along with Harrison, Smith's mother and father took the stand, as did his brother, two sisters, and the usual suspects of thugs and drinking buddies. Smith admitted that he had joined the Klan, but said he had been pressured into it by Clifford Wilson, his employer at the time.

Smith's friends and family made much of the fact that his only previous criminal violation involved a fifteen-dollar fine for hunting on a game preserve without first signing the registration book. But Finch thoroughly discredited the witnesses before the now-biracial jury, and Smith found himself on his way to prison.

The next week, while our family was in California, Clifford Wilson went to trial on murder and arson charges. District Attorney Finch, representing the state, kept his promise to keep prosecuting the Klan until the bitter end. Finch called to the stand FBI agents James Awl and J. L. Martin, who had investigated the Dahmer property after the attack. The agents showed photos of the devastated home and store and identi-

fied a long-barreled .22-caliber revolver as the one found in
the fire-blackened grass in front of the house. Klan informant
Billy Roy Pitts was once more summoned from his witness
protection junket to tell the story of Bowers's "Dahmer project." He also identified the gun as the one he had carried on
the night of January 10, 1966, when he accompanied Clifford
Wilson and the other men on the raid. Pitts said that he had
been a passenger in the same blue Pontiac identified in an earlier trial as part of the drive-by team, and that after the men
reached the Dahmer farm, Cliff Wilson and W. T. Smith had
both opened-fire on the house. Pitts said that Wilson's assign-
ment—as ordered by Sam Bowers—was to set fire to a car and
pickup truck in the Dahmer garage. Pitts admitted that he
didn't actually see Wilson throw the firebombs into the carport, but he did see him running full speed toward it with jugs
of gasoline in both hands.

Ellie Jewel Dahmer also took the stand again, recounting
the horrid events of her husband's murder. She described the
fusillade of gunshots spraying the front of the house and the
tall flames devouring the living room. She described her escape from the rear of the burning house while her husband,
armed with a shotgun, stood guard on the front porch, breathing in fire and smoke. She described her terror, crouched with
her children in the barn behind the house, the concussions of
gun and bomb, uncertain whether her husband was alive or
dead.

"When Mrs. Dahmer takes the stand," the *Laurel Leader-Call*
reported, "the stylized trappings of the courtroom seem to re-
cede in the face of the stock fact that a healthy, hardworking,

businessman and his wife and children were burned out of their home that cold moonlit January morning of 1966."[6] A new image was emerging in the minds of many white Southerners: the sympathetic black victim as symbol of the wounded South.

The disgraced Man of the Year attracted a parade of eighteen character witnesses, not lowlifes and reprobates but upstanding citizens. Along came a distinguished physician, a medical technologist, the principal of Shady Grove High School, a preacher, an insurance salesman, a banker. The president of the Mississippi Junior Chamber of Commerce drove up from Gulfport to vouch for Cliff Wilson's good name, explaining awkwardly that his "reputation for peace and violence was good." When asked whether he knew Wilson had been a member of the Klan, the man said no he didn't, but it wouldn't change his mind if he had. "I don't think you can say a man is violent just because he belongs to a certain organization. I know this man, I've seen him work with retarded children."

But when the jury finally determined itself deadlocked, most observers believed it was the testimony of Wilson's soft-spoken wife that shifted the momentum in his favor. On the night of January 10, 1966, around the time of the attack, Patricia Wilson and her husband had been home together in bed, she told the court in her soft drawl. (The wives of two other indicted Klansmen, Henry Edward DeBoxtel and James Franklin Lyons, would also claim they were home in bed with their husbands. Their men would go free on mistrials, too, later in the year.) But prosecutor James Finch told newspaper reporters and local black leaders that Wilson's day of reckoning was coming someday; he intended to pursue the man until he won a guilty verdict. A new court date was set for January of 1969.

Lawrence Byrd's trial began on November 7, 1968, and ended three working days later. Byrd had admitted in 1966 in a sworn statement to the FBI that he had taken part in the Dahmer killing, although he later claimed he had been forced at gunpoint to sign the affidavit. He had told federal agents that "two or three weeks prior to the Vernon Dahmer burning . . . I attended a special meeting which had been called by Sam Bowers." The meeting was held "on Masonite land in the Bogue Home Swamp, northeast of Laurel," and he had asked Bowers "what they intended to do with Dahmer." According to Byrd, Bowers said that "he was going to take the Dahmer matter into his own hands, and that Dahmer had to be stopped. It was a matter which would have to be decided at the time that the actual hit was made, or possibly during a dry run prior to the hit." Byrd confessed to taking part in the Dahmer murder, adding, "and it has been preying on my mind constantly since that time."[7] The jury spent twelve minutes determining his guilt. Lawrence Byrd was convicted and sentenced to ten years in prison.

True to his word, James Finch got Clifford Wilson back in the courtroom in January of 1969 for the 1966 murder of Vernon Dahmer. Another cast of prominent Mississippians paraded through the courtroom—insurance executives, bankers, medical technologists, business owners, surgeons, the president of the Chamber of Commerce, even my dentist. Mrs. Wilson gave a repeat performance of her previously successful role as demure and faithful helpmate. But the jury wasn't buying it any longer. Finch, who had guided the cases through the long year of convictions and mistrials, collapsed of exhaustion at the end of opening-day arguments, and a young county attorney named James Dukes stepped in for him. Dukes performed admirably. He called numerous FBI agents who identified photographs and sketches made at the scene of the crime and around the Dahmer property and who also convinced the biracial jury that the investigation had been thorough and conclusive. And, of course, Billy Roy Pitts knew the drill by now, having appeared as a witness for the prosecution in nearly a dozen Klan trials. "The last I saw of Clifford Wilson," he said, "until he had finished the job and [was] ready to leave, he was running toward the carport with two jugs of gasoline. He was armed with a pistol and a shotgun." Vernon Dahmer could be heard moaning in agony inside the house. "The place roared with flame."

Pitts added, "I told Cecil Sessum we should save his life, but he snapped, 'Let him die. That's what we came for.'"

On February 1, 1969, Clifford Wilson was convicted of murder and sentenced by Judge Stanton Hall to life in prison. (He would serve only a year before being paroled by Governor William Waller, who had been one of his attorneys in the first trial.) In the end, four men were found guilty of murdering Vernon Dahmer—Cecil Sessum, W. T. Smith, Clifford Wilson, and Lawrence Byrd. Eleven members of the White Knights, including Imperial Wizard Sam Bowers, escaped punishment. (However, thirty years later, in the summer of 1998, Bowers was convicted of murder and arson by a Forrest County jury and sentenced to life in prison.)[8]

The week of Clifford Wilson's conviction, my father was awakened late one night by our assistant pastor, Bert Manning, an energetic young seminarian on loan from New Orleans. My father had hired Manning to help coordinate the youth events of the busy year, and he was currently leading a weekday Bible class called "The *Book of Revelation*: Its Relevance for Today."

"Look out the window, Bob!" Bert shouted. "The fires of judgment are raining down from heaven. The night skies are telling the story! And now Jesus is coming for his church. Oh mercy!"

My father pulled back the blinds of the bedroom window and stared into the dark backyard (The floodlights had burned out and would not be replaced.)

"It all looks pretty normal to me. Maybe you were just having a strange dream."

"You must be looking in the wrong direction," Jones replied. "The fires are burning in the east."

My father put on his robe and bath slippers and walked into the front yard, beyond the lighted porch and the night shadows of the trees, to the end of the sidewalk and the clearing of the street. Above the treeline beyond the Lesters' yard glowed a tunnel of fire, spiraling upward. The eastern horizon was incandescent light, a sea of yellow and red flame.

Looks more like the work of the Klan than the Lord, was my father's first thought. He knew that Bowers, in response to the ongoing Wilson trial, had been heard making threats to even the score. My father told Jones not to panic, but not to expect the Rapture either, while he made a few phone calls.

On the kitchen radio the honky-tonk rhythms of AM 94, the only all-night station in town, had been preempted by a sleepy voice struggling to make sense of his CB. My mother had plugged in the coffee pot and stood by silently.

Parishioner Hap Welch, a young deacon fresh out of Ole Miss, answered on the first ring. Hap was wide awake and moving into action, having just learned that a mile-long freight train filled to capacity with highly flammable containers had plummeted off the rails on its way from New Orleans to Birmingham.

"Looks like Nagasaki over there in Kingston, the sheriff told me. Those little houses just flat disappeared."

Hap Welch was a businessman who intended to revive the state's Republican party on a no-new-taxes platform that included racial moderation. He was on the train crisis immediately, screeching to a halt minutes later in the driveway.

The streets in the Kingston neighborhood were filled with loud and frantic voices. Most of the homes near the tracks were smoldering heaps of plywood and tin. When the Southern Railway freighter derailed in Laurel's black bottom, the container tanks, each holding 23,000 gallons of liquid petroleum, began exploding at thirty-second intervals, with the first blast around 4 a.m. Four of the freight cars ripped open and were propelled a half mile like rockets horizontally in the air. The highway patrol said the blast could be seen in the predawn sky eighty-five miles north in Jackson. On the adjoining streets, fires were erupting everywhere in sight. Ambulances and rescue vehicles wailed in the night, arriving from towns as far away as Gulfport and Picayune. Volunteers from the Red Cross and the Salvation Army had been summoned. The National Guard and the Civil Defense were soon on the scene as well, mobilized by the governor.

By morning, the neighborhood lay in ruins. More than a thousand homes, five churches, six schools, and dozens of small businesses were damaged or destroyed. Two people were dead, and thirty-three were hospitalized with burns and injuries. Property damages would be estimated at three and a half million dollars.

In the days that followed, my father worked with fellow white pastors and reunited with Marcus Cooley, whom he hadn't seen since their visit a year earlier, to provide food, shelter, and consolation—often over the voices of the die-hard bigots who thought Negroes should take care of themselves, even in times like these. The impoverished neighborhood had been exposed for all to see, and my father made sure I saw it too. We had never before witnessed black life firsthand. Like most of the white volunteers, we had only seen the neighborhood from the windows of a passing car. But now we walked together through the blast-littered streets, helping load furniture and other salvaged items onto pickup trucks. The shanties, yards, and gardens continued smoldering for days.

My father may have tried to return black misery to some familiar allegory of the Spirit, as when he addressed the congregation the following Sunday: "I noticed two reactions to the fire and explosion. Some ran in fear; some tried to get closer and were drawn to it. The Bible compares the Holy Spirit to being 'as of fire.' The Spirit of God draws people, and He also repels some. There will always be more drawn than those who run the other way. Can it be said of our church that it is filled with the Holy Spirit? If it is, then we will be drawing people to the Lord Jesus Christ." But decent men could no longer ignore the fires on the other side of the track.

That next week at the Thursday evening youth meeting, the numbers swelled suddenly to four hundred, more than half the student body. Even some black students from Oak Park High School showed up that night in what was perceived by all to be a spontaneous moving of the Spirit. Kids from other churches and denominations showed up too. "We are one in the Spirit, we are one in the Lord," we sang. "We pray that all unity may one day be restored. They will know we are Christians by our love." In the Masonite Room, where my father had bestowed the Man of the Year award on Sam Bowers's favorite hit man, we assembled, black and white together, holding hands and singing, praying for the hurting and the suffering, for the victims of the train explosion, and for the healing of the town. And we would meet again the following week—with more black students in attendance—and every week thereafter until the end of the school year. The apostle's message became our flesh and blood—"so if anyone is in Christ, *there* is a new creation"—reaching all the way to race. No one thought of these Thursday nights at the Pinehurst Hotel as experiments in integration. Charity did not move us, or liberal sentiment—no court order had brought us together. We reveled in the sweet name of Jesus, the deepest human union sealed at Calvary. It was "J-E-S-U-S, J-E-S-U-S (what have you got?), J-E-S-U-S," we cheered in the dimmed light of the chandeliers.

The tensions at First Baptist between the old-timers and the Jesus freaks may have been put on hold by the relocation of the youth events—and all the national and international media attention given to the Klan trials—but it was only a matter of time before the situation in the church reached a crisis. Throughout the spring and fall of 1969, the deacons on the church board went about their usual business—perfunctory worries over budgets, committee and subcommittee coordinations and machinations—while trying hard to ignore the growing numbers of flower children in their midst. A closed-door policy had unofficially existed in congregational life over the years, although no interracial group had tested First Baptist's doors as had happened in other parts of the state. In 1963, the First Baptist Church of Jackson, for example, had been targeted by the "church visits campaign," interracial groups from Tougaloo College that appeared at white churches on Sunday mornings seeking entrance to the worship service. After the first visit, the Jackson church had unanimously voted for a closed-door policy, resolving that the church would "confine its assemblies and fellowships to those other than the Negro race, until such time as cordial relationships could be reestablished."[9] But all of Laurel's interracial gatherings of the year had taken place in public buildings or parks, so our deacons had been spared a formal decision.

In early January of the new decade, 1970, on a Sunday morning dedicated to the theme "Evangelizing the World by the Year 2000," a black girl appeared with a white friend at the eleven o'clock service in the church sanctuary. Her presence sent waves of panic over the church ushers and early arrivals, most of whom were sitting in "a spirit of solemn assembly" in accordance with my father's recent instructions. He would no longer countenance the minutes before church as a time for exchanging fashion compliments and courtesies. "Come into the service with your Bible," he had said. "Read it before service. Bow your head and pray for the pastor. Pray for yourself. Pray for others who are there in our hurting world, many in great spiritual need."

My father was informed of the visitor by the chain-smoking Sam Pack, whose face was a red planet of worry.

After a brief consultation with Hap Welch, the young Republican and church member, my father told the deacons to let the Negro girl stay. The girl had been sitting with her friend in the last row of the main floor for ten minutes.

One parishioner, Josh Redding, had already stormed out of the church—pastor's approval be damned. Josh Redding was an oil man who months later built a segregationist academy in the town of Heidelberg to keep his two daughters and sister's three children from the fate of integrated classrooms. Redding had no intention of "sitting down with niggers in a Christian church," he told my father later, and he headed straight for the parking lot.

Woody Boggum and J. W. Hoge, two retired lawyers who shared Redding's views, preferred a direct challenge to the pastor's decision. "They shagged down the aisle like they'd been stung by wasps"—my father wrote in his journal (now composed in complete sentences)—hoping to corner him as he entered the sanctuary for the service. But my father beat them to the punch, spying the two men through a porthole in the passageway to the pulpit. He let himself through the swinging door before they reached the front. Boggum and Hoge, not ones to accept defeat gracefully, veered around the piano stall and exploded through the side doors into the porte cochere. My father wrote, "They were doing everything to make a statement by their demeanor outside of wearing a sign that said, 'I am a racist and I hate niggers and there is a nigger girl sitting in my church so I am getting the hell out of here. I thought this was going to be a service on reaching the world for Jesus. Who let her in?'" The service proceeded without further incident, and the benediction was delivered.

As the parishioners strolled into the courtyard, Sam Belk pulled my father aside and told him the executive committee had organized a meeting to take stock of the morning's activities. He should get himself to the pastor's seminar room as soon as possible.

With one or two exceptions, the men sitting around the conference table were tired of Jim Crow and the Klan's violent reign, especially the floundering economy as it related to their personal financial prospects. They considered themselves racial moderates. Attorney Sheldon Flowers had prepared affidavits against the White Knights. Hoy Watts volunteered his medical services in a Negro health clinic. Hap Welch advocated increased budget support for colored schools as part of his attempt to demonstrate a little compassionate conservatism. Joe Samuels volunteered his construction company's time to rebuild Negro homes destroyed by fire and arson. Jerry Hurst donated food from his grocery distribution company during the Christmas season. And so my father was caught off guard when the men demanded an apology and said he would need to start rebuilding fences.

"Those two girls came here just to stir up trouble!" Boggum said.

"He's right, Bob." Hoge agreed. "And I'll guarantee you one thing. We're not going to have trouble on my clock."

"I don't know what trouble you're talking about, J. W.," my father said. "You and Woody stormed out the side doors. That's all the trouble I remember. Anyway, there was only one little girl in the church, and she sat in the back and never said a word.

"I'd like to hear a little more about those fences that need mending," he added.

But the deacons said they weren't interested in discussing race relations. My father should offer his apologies to the congregation, preferably from the pulpit the following Sunday. The deacons wanted the matter resolved and put behind.

"As far as I'm concerned, you got some ideas in your head you better get rid of," Sam Belk wheezed.

"You mean like Jesus loving all people?"

"I mean like coloreds in my church," he replied.

"This is Mississippi, not California, Bob," Hoy Watts said calmly. "We're moving along just fine here, but we have our own schedule to keep. Don't try to be a hero."

My father saw Hoy's point. He had once considered himself a gradualist too. He sure didn't think of himself as any kind of hero. But for everything there is a season, a time to keep silent and so forth. And it was time to speak. How could Hoy not see that?

On the other hand, there was something about opening the doors wide just now that seemed implausible, something he couldn't square in his mind: Negroes roaming the rooms and spaces of the church and sanctuary, the exchange of black and white greetings, the admixtures of styles, moods, and smells, the intercourse of two worlds, one world blessed with a certain something—a familiar sensibility and hold on things, he couldn't put his finger on it—the other world, good and decent, beloved of God, but malleable and innocent like a younger brother, an impressionable son. Strange, too, that the exchange didn't seem much of a problem when it occurred at the Pinehurst Hotel—and he couldn't quite put his finger on this either, why some neutral public space made it plausible, but his own church did not. And that troubled him, too, made him feel trapped in a vicious circle of give-and-take—the ethical and the pragmatic, the ought and the maybe-not. But Hoy did have a point, he had to admit, this was Mississippi, not California. He couldn't deny all that that meant, nor the plain fact that he could go only so far. My father never apologized, but the black girl never came back either. He made vague promises to forestall the open doors, and the meeting adjourned.

Occasionally during the following months, a black student would poke his head into the church sanctuary, at least long enough to size up the mood inside. And for a while at least, the Pinehurst Hotel, the football stadium, or the pavilion in

Gardiner Park offered a glimpse of a new South poking its own head in—a place where white and black occasionally sat down together and discovered to their mutual surprise that the world had not gone up in flames. Perhaps we were able to welcome the Jesus movement because the air felt clearer in our Laurel-town, the atmosphere less claustrophobic. I don't think the movement ultimately changed more than a few white students' thinking about race and justice. The energies dissipated over time, and whites and blacks drifted back to their separate worlds. No white people asked black Laurelites forgiveness for the sins of racism, drafted a confession of guilt and reconciliation, discussed the topic in one of our "think-ins." The spiritual energies we did unleash so quickly turned ethereal (those mean old gnostic blues), soaring high above the embattled terrain of Jones County. But the times they were a'changing, and while Jesus might have spared us much misery had he come on down a few years sooner, most of us were probably a little better off that he showed up at all.

With the Dahmer trials over, the Klan's reign of terror in Mississippi had come to an end. Bowers may have temporarily escaped punishment for his role in the firebombing murder, but on June 21, 1970, after several appeal attempts had failed, he began serving a ten-year sentence for conspiracy to kill Mickey Schwerner, James Chaney, and Andrew Goodman. He entered federal prison at McNeil Island, Washington, frustrated and angry. How would the holy war be fought in his absence? The White Knights lay in shambles. Its leaders were now scattered in prisons throughout the country or ostracized in their own hometowns. No one had raised a finger of protest when the FBI began hauling Klansmen off to black graveyards, demanding confessions at gunpoint. Federal desegregation laws were taking shape at every level of the once closed society. There was even serious talk that the Laurel school system would be integrated in the fall. The national landscape was dark and turbulent. The "black soviets" were proving Bowers's greatest fears true as many militant groups became separatist enclaves of anarchy and violence. The media, the academy, the bastions of opinion and intellectual control, had descended into a behavioral sink and begun to rot.[10] Six years of militant vengeance against the heretics had come to this: God's chosen warrior locked up in a foreign land, exiled. The White Knights of the Ku Klux Klan of Mississippi were finished.

And so was my father's loyalty to the old ordeal.

Not that he would be sending in donations to the NAACP any time soon, or inviting the chaplain at Tougaloo College to preach the spring revival. But he'd gotten a glimpse of a bigger world, where faith and freedom no longer wrestled each other for control, and he resolved to make this world his own, even if it took the rest of his life. He had looked around for ways of escape but found none. And then, as anxious of the future as any thirty-five-year-old, but with a heart as big as the moon, he did the best he could. He resolved, before God, to hold up his calling to a standard different from race or custom, and I understand now how hard that must have been: a preacher boy, called to the Big Time—to "lavish Laurel"—only to find himself at ground zero of Mississippi burning, enormous forces of history clashing and clanging, bombs exploding hither and yon, carloads of terrorists speeding along dark highways, children running for cover.

My father's way was never to break the bonds of friendship. He remained loyal to his church, to everyone he was called to serve, whether he liked the person or not. I may have once wished he'd crossed to the other side and joined the ranks of the activist clergy, thrown his body down on Main Street, settled for nothing short of absolute knowledge, and maybe he should have (who can say for sure but God). But one thing's for sure if he had: There would have been no more sermons at First Baptist, no more meat-and-twos with the men at the Manhattan Café. The folks would not have budged an inch. He made compromises. He said what he needed to say to keep his pulpit. But he pointed us toward a more decent religion at the same time. And as the years passed, he grew less inclined to suffer the rebukes of the Reddings and the Belks without kicking up a little more dust, though he would never embarrass a single fool with denunciations meant for an audience. The old-timers were brothers in the Lord in spite of everything, and my father would be the first one at their doorstep when they needed a friend. He made compromises, but he honored more convictions than he betrayed: Faithful to his wife, always a tither, he rooted for the Atlanta Braves before they were champs. He never missed my ball games, as his parents had missed his. He buried the dead, offered consolation to the grieving, and acted in hopes of pleasing God, church, and family in equal measure—and thus acted imperfectly.

As a young father myself, with three children, and yet older than he was in those Laurel years, I sometimes wonder what I would have done. Would I have sacrificed tenure for the sake of the Kingdom, handed over the books and the travels and the unrushed conversations? Would I have made a nod toward the new, despite all the old baggage and the fears of recrimination?

I once asked my mother what she remembered of Laurel. "There was such an emphasis on social things. So many social pressures."

"Do you remember the Klan, the nights when the street-lights were turned off, dad's despair, all that?"

"You always wanted a brother, I remember." Our fears forged separate worlds, apparent only now, after years of trying to see them as one, as shared memories, hopes, and dreams. Which is not to say I haven't constructed perspectives on the man suitable to my own being-in-the-world—you are holding the proof—and shifted the anxiety of influence slightly in my favor. But after a while, after the claims of freedom had been staked and the battles fought, there came to me a notion—not in a sudden moment but as a slow turning—that love had always been there, love as heavy as rain, the kind that can wash the air clean or leave you panting like a dog, but love it was still, nothing else but love, everywhere love. The face-to-face encounters that always ruined a good meal gave way to sports talk, the esoterica of the Deep South towns of our past, and a comforting stillness. We achieved our own second naïveté, my father and I, the welcome company of the mundane that lies beyond resentment and anger. The grace that got us through the Laurel years would not fail even later. The easy silences of old friends.

14

Once You Go Black

By the end of 1969, two years after we moved to Laurel, the Mississippi of burning crosses, segregated drinking fountains, and organized white resistance was fast going with the wind. "The movement had won significant victories," the historian John Dittmer wrote in his luminous book *Local People: The Civil Rights Movement in Mississippi*, clear evidence that a "degree of civility had come to the Magnolia State."[1] In early 1964, fewer than 7,000 of the state's 450,000 blacks were eligible to vote. Now, in 1969, more than a quarter of a million were registered.[2] In cities like Jackson, Meridian, Greenville, Hattiesburg, and

Laurel too, you saw blacks eating in white-owned restaurants—maybe not in catfish camps or coffee shops but in chains like Stuckey's or Toddle House or Morrison's Cafeteria. Blacks could stay in most local motels and patronize public libraries. They could even leave their perch in the cinema balcony for the seats below. (My friends and I took advantage of the opportunity and claimed the front row upstairs for ourselves.)

However, Dittmer's hopefulness is a cautious one. The new openness resided largely in the realm of legal protections and public accommodations, of getting into once forbidden spaces, of gaining access. Gaining access was surely no small thing if you'd been denied it, but it wasn't quite the promised land Dr. King had spied either. In fact, white Mississippians shared a naughty little secret: Everyday practices had changed very little.

My grandma Lilly complained of the relaxed racial codes and customs that had once made the South great. Federal courts could rewrite the books all they wanted, she wasn't going to change her ways. If a nigra man came to the front door selling lady peas or blackberries, she let him know where to find her: at the side entrance where he belonged, between the mulberry bushes—Lyndon Johnson be damned. Blacks would forever remain "nigras" in her mind, only a slight demurral on the word "niggers," which tempting though it may have been to use, had become popularly affiliated with white trash and ill breeding. "Lordy, Lordy!" she would moan if she saw a black man giving his opinion on the nightly news. A nigra had no business talking with a stiff upper lip like he was some kind of Philadelphia lawyer.

My grandfather, Howard Marsh, grew irritable and moody and plotted his escape from west Jackson. A Negro family had purchased a home on Robinson Avenue, quite a few blocks away from Buena Vista Boulevard but close enough for him to smell danger. He got angry one afternoon when he found me listening to soul music in the pool house.

"Don't ever listen to that again," he said, seizing the transistor radio and turning the dial.

"I love soul," I snapped back, as much to compensate for my humiliation as to argue the point. "It's my favorite. I listen to it all the time in Laurel," and I started singing "Hot Fun in the Summertime" in a nervous falsetto.

He stared at me, cracked his lighter open against his wrist, and flicked the starter several times, getting no fire. He wanted to come down hard, I could see it in his eyes. But he checked himself and carried his drink and smoking pipe out to the patio.

In 1974, Howard bought some property in a new development called Plantation Shores, "an elite exclusive community," announced the modest signage posted on two-by-fours alongside State Highway 49. Howard claimed that one day he and Liz would build a house by the lake, that the mobile home was just temporary. But the fact is he enjoyed life in a trailer; it made him feel like he was living in a fish camp, fishing being what he liked best. In 1977, they purchased a second trailer to make a double-wide, which gave them enough room for a bar and cocktail tables. The house by the lake remained unbuilt. By the time Howard died of a stroke in 1982, the trailers had been ruined by mildew, vaguely redolent of rodent carcasses and dog urine. The dense stands of kudzu and scrub pine had overgrown the yard and driveway. My grandfather used to joke about how the coloreds who'd bought his house in west Jackson had stocked the pool with catfish, but this same grandfather died in a Jim Crow trailer park because he liked the notion of living in a fish camp.

My uncle Phinn still believed in the curse of Ham, the Old Testament story recast by Southern segregationists as the definitive account of white supremacy. According to Genesis, the patriarch Noah had fallen into a drunken stupor, and when he woke up, he cursed Ham, who had discovered his father's nakedness, and his son Canaan. "A servant of servants shall he be unto his brother," declared Noah. That's it as far as the story in Genesis goes, and you would think it an unlikely proof-text for the biblical defense of white supremacy. But in Phinn's mind—as in the mind of many Southern whites—Noah had also marked his son with dark skin, condemning the boy and his descendants to perpetual servitude. All the fuss about Negro advancement was a waste of time as far as he was concerned. The sharecroppers who worked his Louisiana plantation lived in shanties befitting the accursed. No court order or NAACP resolution could rewrite sacred history or improve their lives.

Everyday rituals were pretty much the same. Tuesdays at the county fair remained "nigger nights." Eleven o'clock Sunday morning was the most segregated hour of the week. In the estimation of many white folks, Martin Luther King was still Martin Luther Koon. If a Negro man raked or mowed our yard, he could expect his lunch on the back porch. If he

needed to relieve himself, he could go off in the woods somewhere. Nettie, our maid, sat in the backseat of our car on the
way home from work. She took a bus in the mornings.
Clearly, there were many significant victories the movement
had not won.

In October of 1969, in the new school year filled with "'out
of sight' farm retreats, prayer and study groups, lectures, and
question and answer sessions with visiting speakers," the U.S.
Supreme Court in the case of *Alexander v. Holmes County* once
again turned its attention to school desegregation in Mississippi. To avoid compliance with the 1954 *Brown v. Board* decision, public school districts over the years had seized upon the
phrase "all deliberate speed" as a means of deferring integration as long as possible, hoping the federal government would
tire of the issue or just forget about it, hoping that some new
domestic or foreign crisis would come along—as was the case
with the Vietnam student protests—and seize the spotlight in
its place. Or perhaps even Jesus would return to rapture his
Church and establish the eternal, separate-but-equal Kingdom. (Byron de la Beckwith, the Klan killer of civil rights
leader Medgar Evers, may have been extreme in his kookiness,
but he spoke for many white Christians when he pledged himself "to believe in segregation like I believe in God." "And fur-
thermore, when I die," seethed the demented Episcopalian,
"you'll find me in a part of Heaven that has a sign saying, 'FOR
WHITES ONLY!', and, if I go to Hades—I'm going to raise
Hell all over Hades 'til I get in the WHITE SECTION OF
HADES!"[3]

Ten years after *Brown*, with not a single school district integrated in Mississippi—and again no Rapture either—the 1964
Civil Rights Act ordered desegregation of all public schools
receiving federal aid. The Civil Rights Act also permitted parents to send their children to any school they desired. In the
so-called Freedom of Choice Plan, black children could enroll
in white schools, but only a handful of black families in Mississippi participated in the plan. The results for the children
were nightmarish: Ridicule, harassment, playground mug-
gings, racial taunts, were all part of the daily grind.[4]

But the U.S. Supreme Court would put an end to clever cir-
cumventions of the law and whatever new strategies of nullifi-
cation and interposition might be imagined. *Alexander v. Holmes
County* was followed by the specific mandate of the Fifth U.S.
Circuit Court of Appeals on December 2, 1969, ordering sixteen school districts to integrate immediately. The Laurel
school system was one of those named—to be integrated from
top to bottom, "massively." In ruling against the State of Mississippi, Judge Walter L. Nixon of U.S. District Court in Jackson
issued the order for a comprehensively redesigned "unitary
non-discriminatory school system," "The school board is thus
directed to immediately take the necessary steps to implement
this plan for senior and junior high students for the 1970–1971
school session," read the decision.[5] The ruling required immediate integration of public schools in accordance with fair and
nondiscriminatory reassignments of teachers and administrators, as well as a large number of capital expenditures: sidewalks, crossing signals, traffic lights, barriers at railroad tracks
to prevent children from harm when crossing over into unfa-

miliar territory, fences to prevent children from crossing a heavily trafficked street at a place other than the designated crossing, a company of crossing guards, and the buses.

Hoping against hope, state officials gave the politics of deferral one more desperate push, making last-minute appeals for clemency, filing complaints with all federal agencies involved, and requesting more time (preferably of the all-deliberate-speed variety). Mississippi Attorney General A. F. Sumner launched a statewide move to block National Education Association observers from checking on school desegregation, and he set off on "an inspection tour" of the state of Minnesota (home of the despised racemonger Hubert Humphrey). His intention was to call attention to Northern hypocrisy, specifically by asking why the Minneapolis–St. Paul area "can operate neighborhood schools that aren't racially balanced and Mississippi cannot."[6] (The IRS answered the attorney general's stiff-arm by revoking the tax-exempt status for all private schools that refused to adopt racially nondiscriminatory admission policies.) At the same time, the Citizens' Council, the middle-class organization founded in 1954 to preserve the separation of the races, enjoyed a sudden burst of moral energy after several years of floundering efforts. Council Secretary Robert Patterson was happy to find himself back in the spotlight. "It is indeed sickening to hear some of our brain-washed educated people whine, 'It's inevitable. There's nothing we can do. We have lost,'" he would say once again.[7] Next door, George C. Wallace was instructing Alabama parents to defy the federal court order and proceed with business as usual.

It was not until the first week of September 1970, with all legal courts of appeals finally exhausted—and my seventh-grade year temporarily on hold—that state officials finally threw in the towel. "This [Supreme Court] plan is not in accordance with the thinking of many people and there is great doubt in many quarters if so-called quality education can be maintained," wrote editorialist Ralph Hays in the *Leader-Call*. But the fact remained that "either by court order, or voluntarily, we will be operating our schools in accordance with federal laws which require total de-segregation." The Supreme Court ruling could not be finessed to suit our preferences. Mississippi segregation was history.[8]

According to Judge Nixon's plan, the city's three junior high schools would be consolidated in compliance with strict guidelines determined by the U.S. district court. The plan stipulated that seventh graders from white neighborhoods in east-central Laurel and from black neighborhoods in south Laurel be assigned to a brownstone fortress once known as Gardiner Elementary, two blocks south of Jones Junior High School—even though the number of students exceeded the number of desks in any single school building. Judge Nixon explained in his September decision, "All school construction and site selection (including the location of any temporary classrooms) in the system shall be done in a manner which will prevent the recurrence of the dual school structure once this desegregation plan is implemented." In other words, since neither the judge nor local officials could figure out what to do with us, we were to be dumped into one overcrowded building with a good-luck wish and a pat on the back.

There was an even darker side to the Nixon plan. Black principals, with solid credentials and years of experience in educational leadership, were reassigned to the classroom or to the guidance counselor's office, or if they were lucky, to the position of vice principal. Black head coaches would become assistant coaches. Irving Morrell, an All-American center while at Grambling University, had won three district championships as head coach at Oak Park High with an overall record of 77 to 5. Thanks to the U.S. Supreme Court, he became the proud manager of the seventh- and eight-grade hoopsters, the team I played on. He grew surly and mean, snarled at our developing talents, and still won every game and tournament for the next two years.

With the federal government's final ruling now standing before us, Mayor Bill Patrick and my father, along with school board members and civic leaders, rounded up a hundred or so parents and held a public rally at Watkins High School. The hope was to put the best face possible on the situation and form a core group of supportive white Laurelites. Many feared that their children would be greeted the first day of school by Negro mobs and harassed or beaten on the playgrounds—in other words, the same kind of "welcome" whites had extended to the few black kids who'd integrated under the 1964 Freedom of Choice plan. Newspapers in Laurel and Jackson—the dailies we had access to—ran regular articles recounting the acts of violence against white students in the South: "Unrest Grips High Schools in Mobile," "White Girls Terrorized," "Racial Violence Erupts in Two Louisiana Towns," "Rankin County Lawmen Arrest Black Students."

I had my own fears too. Mother and I went to Jackson to see an orthodontist about my teeth. I'd learned that the cause of my vast dental complexities was four congenitally missing teeth—two on top, two on the bottom—as well as the presence of a frenum, a tentacle-like muscle separating my two front teeth (and along with the missing four teeth giving me the look of a jack-o-lantern), which would have to removed. I'd be treated to years of retainers, braces, caps, bridges, and surgical maneuvers around bicuspids and through gaps. After the appointment, my mother and I stopped by Lillian's house for ham sandwiches and peach pie. A boy who lived next door, a sixth-grader at the "seg academy" east of town, came over to play before supper. He asked me where I was going to school in Laurel, and when I told him, he laughed and said I could expect a knife in the gut.

"You're crazy to be going to school with niggers," he said. "When they're done with you, you'll be looking like a newspaper in a hamster cage."

Lillian was concerned too. After supper, she gave my mother a copy of Tom Brady's *Black Monday*, which Brady himself had given to my grandfather when the book was published in 1954. Lillian told my mother she wasn't taking integration seriously enough. "You and Bob must read this book before making up your mind," she said, gripping the book tightly with her two hands.

Tom Brady was the Ivy League–educated attorney and Mississippi Supreme Court justice widely regarded as the most eloquent and fair-minded defender of the Southern Way of Life. "The tap roots of our social, political and economic or-

ders are buried deep in the oozes of antiquity," he wrote in
Black Monday. If you look carefully there, he explained, deep in
antiquity's oozes, you'll discover three distinct races of human
beings: the "Great White Race, Homo Caucasius," "Homo
Mongoloideus," and "Homo Africanus." In fact, the three
sprang to life around the same time and evolved alongside
each other, although Homo Africanus was separated from
Homo Caucasius by "unconquerable seas" and "an impassable
desert barrier." But while Homo Caucasius and Homo Mongoloideus improved themselves steadily over time, enduring
"the throes of change and growth," the Negro remained "hidden in the steaming jungle, afraid of his very shadow," no
more evolved than "the modern lizard." "Clothed only in a
loin cloth," Brady wrote, "with a churinga stone about his
neck, his teeth sharpened by rough rocks so that they can
more easily tear human flesh, he squats and utilizes the great
discovery he has made, namely that the point of his green
spear can be hardened by a flame of fire. Here we find the
Negro, only one-half step from the primordial brute. . . .
These are the melancholy facts, and they cannot be refuted."[9]

This being the case—that "the mental inferiority of the
Negro to the white is an established fact"—Brady raised the
question of why Negroes would even want to integrate in
white schools. He knew why. "The communist leaders of this
world are not fools. They know a mongrelized race is an ignorant, weak, easily conquered race." The communists' plan was
to infiltrate liberal political organizations under the guise of
compassion—Brady listed a hundred and twenty-five such
compassionate organizations—and together convince Ne-

groes that integration offered quick and easy access to an overall racial upgrade (all the while "grading down" God-fearing white Southerners in the process). So the stakes could not have been higher. Nothing less than the fate of Homo Caucasius was hanging in the balance, nothing less than Western Civilization. "You cannot place little white and Negro children together in class rooms and not have integration," Tom Brady concluded. "They will sing together, dance together, eat together and play together. They will grow up together and the sensitivity of the white children will be dulled. . . . This is the way it has worked out in the North. This is the way the N.A.A.C.P. wants it to work out in the South and that is what Russia wants."[10] My mother slipped *Black Monday* in her red-vinyl purse and we kissed Lillian goodbye.

And yet here they were, white parents born and raised in the midcentury Jim Crow South, gathered in the Watkins High School gym and pledging to set their children loose on Tom Brady's "mongrelization turnpike." In the audience were my mom and dad; Frank and Faith Harper, owners of a furniture store and a fashion boutique; Dennis and Ingrid Womach, a former Alabama gridiron star and his debutante wife; Bud and Boddette Pippin, a car salesman and his beautician wife; Frank and Helen Jenkins, a circuit court judge and a historian; Mitch and Francis Devota, a Masonite foreman and a mother of six; Abe and Rachel Steiner, a Jewish businessman and a housewife; assistant district attorney and his wife, Margaret Ann; and others, too, whose names are forgotten: bankers, poultry plant operators, tire salesmen, oil tycoons, catfish farmers, museum curators, barbers, and construction workers.

"The faculty of the Laurel City Schools is facing the greatest challenge this year in the history of schools," school board member Wilson Howard told the audience. "It is up to each of you to put forth a one hundred percent effort beginning with the first day of classes. The school board is anxious to preserve public education and it depends on you, the teachers and parents, to do the job this year."[11] The mayor promised his white constituents there'd be no foolishness on his clock, no "hardcore anarchists" tolerated. A professor from the state university in Hattiesburg ruminated on the telltale signs of student unruliness and aggression, lamenting the fact that "the values we were taught, such as self-discipline and the satisfaction of achievement, are no longer the values of the generation today." Concerned parent Brenda Flowers, wearing an ankle-length red, white, and blue maxi, led the audience in the Pledge of Allegiance. Before he offered the benediction, my father suggested to polite applause that the three Rs of "reading, 'riting, and 'rithmetic" be changed to "respect, responsibility, and religion."

Many whites thought Laurel would have gotten to this day sooner had "the communists not come to town" a few years earlier.[12] "Time to move on," was the sentiment preferred, and we would do so "peacefully and orderly" as President Nixon wanted. As far as the wealthy Laurelites who traveled to New York and Europe were concerned, they were tired of impolite questions about tortures and lynchings and disappeared children. If integration was the price of respectability, then so be it.

And after all, the year was 1970. The Black Power movement may have scared the living daylights out of us in 1966, when Stokely stood in the town square of Greenwood and announced that "every courthouse in Mississippi should be burnt down tomorrow so we can get rid of the dirt."[13] But at this late hour, the celebration of all things sub-Saharan and African had entered the pop-cultural mainstream in far less menacing forms, trickling down even to Jones County tastes in fashion and music. The fear of Stokely, Rap, and a "third world coalition of revolutionaries" had given way to platform shoes, perms, and Sly and the Family Stone.

Still, the parents gathered in Watkins High gym were ready to get on with it. They might not have revised their opinions of Martin Luther King or the civil rights movement; they may have even already made the mental turn toward the party of Reagan in order to spite the Great Society villains; but they were doing the right thing as far as it went at sunset in the Jim Crow South. My mother's sister in Louisiana wrote us a letter:

> How is ya'lls school situation? Yesterday the School Superintendent sent a paper home to us telling about the complete integration this next year—if not sooner! They are turning the Negro high school over into a Vocational School. Grades 1–2 and 9–12 go to the white school and the others to the colored school. We have a bunch of people who are working on a private school. Phinn and I would love to see a Christian day school. Pray for us about the whole matter.

In fact, they would see a Christian school in no time at all. An aluminum-sided building was thrown together in a Delta hamlet thirty miles from their plantation—aluminum being the preferred material of the seg academies—and their three school-age children were taught by a recent Bob Jones graduate.

Most towns in our neck of the woods were going the way of Josh Redding's Heidelberg Academy, having conceded defeat to federal desegregation laws, and were busy filing "Christian day school" charters, searching the church rolls for qualified or semiqualified teachers, raising money for books and buildings, and rallying white families around the cause of segregation private-sector style. Throughout the South, as the daily news reports indicated, many public schools were shutting down altogether—in Mobile, Memphis, Bogalusa, and Houston—fearing riots and violent demonstrations. But in Laurel, business and civic leaders, white and black, were determined to see integration through. When a group of parents calling themselves the Laurel Christian Academy Council sent out a survey to determine the anticipated enrollment for a segregationist school (we needed a more convenient location than Heidelberg, was the thinking), it failed to receive enough interest to fill up a single grade.

No one in my parents' circle held liberal positions on racial matters, including my parents. My father did not organize study groups on the Bible and integration, nor mention the subject directly in his sermons or in any of his weekly columns in the church bulletin. He was still a good Baptist boy in this respect, keeping his religion and his politics separate. A day would come when he would speak out clearly and pay up personally, as far as race went. In a few years he would welcome a black man down the aisle with a hug, and preach the sermon "Amazing Grace for Every Race" on the Sunday of the convert's baptism. Even later, he would celebrate the wedding of an interracial couple in his congregation and become the black husband's jogging partner. But for now, it was enough that the old proof texts of separate-but-equal had finally grown tired and empty.

Besides, too many of our fellow Christians around the nation—and evangelicals at that—were criticizing our behavior. "The man who runs a Jim Crow church is an enemy of Christ, and there's no getting around it," wrote a Christian journalist in Ohio. The federal government we could still vilify, for reasons painfully obvious in a state where "Hell No, I Won't Forget!" bumper stickers could still be bought at most gas stations. But the rebukes of evangelical leaders like Billy Graham and Carl F. H. Henry, or American missionaries overseas, made my father wince with shame. "Our people listen to the radio, they read the newspaper," wrote a Southern Baptist missionary in Ghana. "And some even have television. They know what is happening today. It is impossible to explain why a black person can't worship in a Baptist church in America when you send us out here to tell him that Jesus loves them."[14] Carl Henry, editor of the conservative magazine *Christianity Today*, had written in a recent book, "All Christians should strive to replace discriminatory laws by non-discriminatory laws," while reassuring readers of his ultimate loyalty to "the dynamic of supernatural *regeneration* and *sanctification*." In other words, if you're a born-again Christian, you better show some love for your black brothers and sisters.

Then there was the example of fellow Southerner Billy Graham, the most ferocious soul-winner in Christian memory, refusing to speak to segregated audiences. Graham had taken the position that the Holy Bible condemned racial discrimination—the same red-leather King James version he waved in the air night after night. Since his 1953 evangelistic crusades in Chattanooga, when he tore down the dividing ropes himself, Graham had refused segregated audiences. Not too long after the Chatanooga services, he had told Jackson Christians that their two biggest problems were illegal liquor and racial inequality.[15] Billy Graham, to whom my father attributed his own salvation—certainly much more than Bobby Kennedy or Lyndon Johnson—stirred his uneasy conscience into a willingness to change, if not to see change as God-ordained. "The ground at the foot of the cross is level," Graham said. "It touches my heart when I see whites stand shoulder to shoulder with blacks at the foot of the cross."[16]

My father convened a family meeting one afternoon in the first week of September, which made me curious because we never had family meetings. We gathered around the marble-top coffee table in the living room and sat in the upholstered chairs. My parent's Bible lay on the table in front of us.

My father began. "Charles, I'm sure you've heard a lot about the school situation in town. We haven't talked much about it, I know, but your mother and I thought that we should spend a little time today sharing our feelings, making sure we're all together on the thing."

My mother was nodding her head and looking directly at my father.

"I know you don't like it when we say this," my father continued, "but your mother and I love you more than anything else in the world. We want nothing but the best for you. We love you more than life itself, if you can believe that—and if you can forgive me for sounding like corny old dad. But I've especially come to realize in the past year that I would give everything I have for your happiness, anything at all. And that's why I want us all to be very clear about how we feel."

I nodded, too.

"There is no question but that the Lord has led us to Laurel and put us in this situation for a purpose. There is no question that God has a will for us here, but doing His will does not come easily—this much I now know for sure. God sends us, He puts us, He keeps us, then He moves us. You've heard me say this before on Sunday mornings. But if we try to get in the way when God is working in our circumstances, we can get into serious trouble. All of this may sound like preaching, and I'm sorry if it does, because I don't mean it to be. I want to say something very real, right now. I want to say that after a season of soul-searching, your mother and I have reached the decision that God wants us to stay in the school system, to be part of all that is good in this town."

My mother shifted in her seat, holding the arms of the chair with two hands.

"Now, I've personally spoken with leaders from both races. I've studied the whole situation, given it a hundred and ten percent of my attention, and I am confident—as are the men I've talked to—that we'll make the adjustment safely and smoothly. But, son, here's the thing I want to you to understand. You're the person who'll be going to the new school, not me or mom. It's easy for us to sound upbeat, but you're the key player. I say this because if you have any reservations about going, any whatsoever, we will happily—and I mean happily!—drive you every morning to the Heidelberg Academy."

I thought of the school, an aluminum building on a treeless plain in a forlorn red-hilled hamlet fifteen miles away, with not enough boys in the entire junior high to field a football team. But I also thought about Lilly's next-door neighbor, and his forecast of a knife in the gut. But then I thought of something else. I thought of a trip my elementary school had taken a year earlier. Mrs. Grantham, the principal at Mason Elementary, had accepted an invitation for our choir to sing at Sandy Gavin, a black elementary school in southeast Laurel. On a cold morning in early March, we were welcomed by three hundred black children sitting quietly in metal folding chairs. We sang a medley of patriotic songs that concluded in a dramatic rendition of "This Is My Country." Pledging our allegiance to America the bold, to have and to hold, our hands swept the circumference of our circle, synchronized for just the right effect. Mine, not yours. But the black children had been coached, too. When the assembly came to an end, and my classmates and I had recessed down the center aisle to board the bus, we were greeted with a standing ovation that did not end until the last one of us had left the building. I thought about those three hundred buffed and scrubbed black kids sitting straight in the chairs, smiling like little aristocrats, and I decided I'd take my chances in Laurel.

"I want to go to Jones," I told my father.

"That's great, son. I'm proud of you, mother and I are really proud."

She offered me a smile and reached over and pressed my hand softly.

"But let me just tell you one more time," my father said. "You don't have to do this. Josh Redding has made it clear to me that a scholarship is available if you want to go to the academy."

"I don't want to go out there," I said.

"Okay then," my father said resolutely. He turned to my mother. "Myra, will you read us a verse, and then I'll pray."

My mother picked up her Bible and thumbed for a passage.

"I've been spending a lot of time in Romans lately," she explained, "so I'll think I'll read something from there, the eighth chapter. God has really spoken to me in these verses lately." She smoothed the pages with her fingers. "'Who shall separate us from the love of Christ?'" she read. "'Shall tribulation, or distress, or persecution, or famine, or nakedness, or peril, or sword? As it is written, "For thy sake we are killed all the day long; we are accounted as sheep for the slaughter." Nay in all these things we are more than conquerors through him that loved us. For I am persuaded, that neither death, nor life, nor angels, nor principalities, nor powers, nor things present, nor things to come, nor height, nor depth, nor any other creature, shall be able to separate us from the love of God, which is in Christ Jesus our Lord.'"

Tears streamed down my mother's face as she read, and when she finished, she began to sob and covered her face with her hands. Dad wrapped her in his arms, and then I embraced the two of them, and we stood together for a moment in silence. When my mother reached down and put her hands on my shoulder, I saw that her mascara was running in black streaks from her eyes. I laughed out loud, "You look like you're wearing a Mardi Gras mask," and she and my father laughed, too. But it was really more like a mask coming off, after so many years of wear, and it just cracked me up to see it, and it cracked my parents up too, and after a few more minutes together we were still standing in a circle laughing, laughing so loud that if you didn't know us any better, you'd have thought we were the weirdest people in the world. My father was laughing so hard he even forgot to pray.

On September 8, 1970, on a sweltering hot morning, the public schools integrated, not only in Laurel but throughout the South. "School bells rang in a new era today," the UPI wire announced. "Thousands of children began classes under new integration plans.[17]

My father drove me to school in our new car—a 1970 Impala, chocolate brown this time, with an interior cabin big enough for a small army. The temperature outside was rising fast toward the day's high of 98 degrees, but I wore a thick winter coat and a new pair of Levis—the non-prewashed kind that smelled like wet hay and felt as heavy as armor. When my father asked me why I was wearing the coat, I told him I was trying to get some extra padding in case I was attacked. But once inside the school building, it became obvious that the black kids were worried, too—no doubt their friends and neighbors had been talking to them about burning crosses and Molotov cocktails. The two races marched to class in appreciation of the moment, the hallways silent except for the sound of Keds and Converses sliding along tile floors. I may have been fearing a mob of thirteen-year-old Panthers—trained in the trash-littered hallways of the Nam-Cam Housing Projects near the Laurel fairgrounds—but the black kids could not have forgotten the not-so-long-ago days of Klan violence and mayhem. I hung up the winter coat in my assigned locker, which happened to be between the lockers of two black kids with the same last name as mine: to my left, a girl wearing a shiny blue dress named Angela; to my right, a boy named Deon, who reached out and shook my hand when he saw me. The next day, I left the winter coat at home.

With a wretched decade behind us at last, we were finally all there together in Gardiner seventh grade: sons and daughters of Klansmen and civil rights activists, of circuit clerks and deputy sheriffs, of black militants and Citizens' Councilors, of society matrons and union organizers. Isaac Buckley, whose father Travis Buckley had once been described in a *Time* magazine profile of the Klan as "a cocky, stocky, pugnacious little Klansman with jug ears," was there too. Isaac was a pathetic child, much too old for his grade, who smelled of wild onions. Having been harassed for years by his white classmates, Isaac made a surprising discovery. He liked black kids better. They didn't meet his idiosyncrasies with cruelty. His new friends were Unkgang Harrison and Flip Freeman, muscle-riddled boys who thought nothing of Isaac's oversized clothes, his scarred face and body odor, or his Klan father.

As the days wore on, the presence of the black children, who made up 45 percent of the student body, seemed a vague, if not slightly pleasing, curiosity. Gardiner Park became our playing field; the dark gullies, green meadows, and clusters of crepe myrtle and azalea serving as background for a Citizens' Councilor's nightmare—black and white kids rubbing shoulders, defamations of natural law, Anglo-Saxon Christian hegemony crumbling all around. We ran in a thousand different directions, swarmed together in packs, divided into a thousand more singularities, small groups and powwows, laughed and shrieked, and sometimes stopped and stared at each other in wonder.

Don't misunderstand me. Plenty of white parents were still steaming mad, blaming my family and the other white moderates for the "monumental mess" in Laurel, as one father wrote in a letter to the *Leader-Call* editor. "Those of us who have done all we could to sound the alarm before it was too late would appreciate the community leaders and the press showing the courage to call the schools by their proper name, GOVERNMENT SCHOOLS." School administrators had been pressed at the eleventh hour to give much thought to class selections. You might get us into the same building, some parents squeaked, but you won't get us into the same rooms. Separate but equal could be haggled over with metaphysical precision.

Question: How many nigra children can fit in the eye of a needle?

Answer: Zero, if my sandy-haired daughter was in there first.

And so for the first year of the desegregated school system, 1970–1971, blacks and whites shared a common school house and yard but not much more. We met briefly in hallways and in the lunchroom, or at recess on the playground or in the park behind the school, sitting at our separate tables in nearly separate worlds and classrooms. Administrators claimed they were just trying to work out the particulars, to measure our mutual capabilities and prior training so as to maintain quality education for both races.

But it wasn't long before this was finished too. There was no escaping the inevitable: All parts of school life would have to comply with the desegregation mandates. And at least from my eight-grade perspective the following year, who would want to escape, anyway? I was having so much fun.

All three of my Fighting Yellow Jackets sports teams at Jones Junior High won championships, thanks to the swift and graceful Joe Porter, who scored touchdowns and jump shots at will, shattered junior high records in the 50, the 100, the 220, and the pole vault—or any other track-and-field event he felt like entering. As a tailback, Joe possessed a perfect hesitation step in the manner of Franco Harris or Walter Peyton, freezing the defense the split second he spotted the one hole available to penetrate. Once clear of the defensive line, he sprinted to the goal line with a stride so even you could draw parallel lines from the forward progress of his head and the grass beneath his feet.

After seeing Joe score four touchdowns in the first game of the season, one of our church members whose child was on the team told my father, "I wouldn't want the boy in my dining room, but I sure like the way he handles that football." But I had a different take on the matter. I wanted to be Joe Porter.

Joe also started in the defensive backfield, which was where I played, and the two of us exchanged tips on the opposing players and soul-shakes after blocked passes and interceptions. Joe never criticized me when I got burned on a touchdown pass. He'd even threaten the black guys on the other teams if they hit me late or tried to rip out my mouthguard in the pushing and shoving going on beneath a pileup. His move to the goal in basketball was a thing of beauty; I could not believe how he kept his body suspended in air, or the way he turned and twisted effortlessly until he was wide open for the easy layup. I'd always been known as a ball-hog by my white friends, never saw a jump shot I didn't like, they said, but I loved passing the ball to Joe as he glided into the lane, making the perimeter-to-post transaction as smooth as silk. In track, I handed him the baton on the 220 relay, and even occasionally gained ground on my rival third legs. Whether I reached Joe a few steps ahead or a few steps behind, his custom was to thank me for the baton. "That's good, thanks." And then dust. Joe gave me the nickname "Nanu"—the guy in the Disney movie who became the world's greatest athlete—which was a nice touch, since I was only the county's fastest white boy.

After games or track meets in the late afternoons, the cheerleaders and members of the pep squad waited for us outside the locker room. We'd take our time in the shower, scrubbing our chests, armpits, and crotches like the sky was the limit. We'd bark like hyenas if a little too much scrubbing was discovered going on, or if the pubescent body just revved up by itself. Sometimes even, with the hot water raining down on my stomach and thighs, I might reach a perfect place somewhere between flaccidity and arousal—a magnificent tumescence where I felt both expanded and relaxed. And while I might have been thinking of girls, who elicited visceral cravings while remaining mostly abstract pleasures (though a few of my teammates claimed otherwise), I was surrounded by boys, stealing glimpses at each other and trying not to get caught. We dressed with a dandy's care—it didn't matter we wore tattered scrimmage jerseys and a pair of blue jeans. We combed and brushed and picked our hair, constantly pushing our way into the view of the narrow mirror. I started keeping a pick in my back pocket the way Joe did, exposing the black rubber handle and its accompanying clenched fist, even though my hair was fine and dry. When our grooming was finished, we exited the locker room into the fading autumn light, in some order approximating the afternoon's big achievers— Joe always at the head—into the cheers of the awaiting crowd, and then into the arms of our girlfriends, waving goodbye as we walked toward our separate neighborhoods.

Jerome Johnson sashayed through the halls of Jones Junior High with his face buried in a book, raising his eyebrows at the stringy-haired philistines it was now his fate to endure. Jerome read the classics, "unabridged." He read Rousseau and Mills and W.E.B. Du Bois. He read the *Encyclopedia Britannica* from A to Z. In cool weather he swept a paisley scarf around his neck and sported a black beret. His booming voice overwhelmed any discussion, hallway or lunchroom conversation, full of passion and tumult. He held forth on Greek civilization or the plight of the English working class. He had no intellectual equal, he made clear, shaking his head in disbelief at our gargled responses to some obligatory short story by O. Henry. As far as Jerome was concerned, he'd thought the matter through—whatever we were discussing—with reference to other more important writers and to this theory or that, and he offered his explanations in a manner that silenced us completely. Any notions we white kids still harbored of our superior intelligence lay in ruins by the end of the fall.

Jerome was not an unfriendly child. He was friendly in a way that measured kindness against strength, leaving little room for more than a reciprocating nod of the head. He didn't need cheap retorts like "it's a scientific or historical fact" thrown in as the desperate trump card in a class discussion. He could take you through the problem backward and forward until you were so dizzy you couldn't see straight.

Jerome wrote his fall book review on *War and Peace* (the unabridged version, he told us more than once). He read his presentation from a typed manuscript, taking the entire hour. A few days later, after staggering through a summary of *The Babe Ruth Story*, I would never again mistake the golden-back biographies for classics.

I said Jerome had no intellectual equal. The truth is he had no equal among the white kids. Among his own race prowled his nemesis, Zeke Mays. Zeke was edgy, unforgiving, black as tar. He despised Jerome as much as he despised me and the rest of us "sorry-ass white kids." His father was the Reverend A. M. Mays of the Zion Street African Methodist Episcopal

Church, who'd gone on record with his criticism of the Reverend Allan Johnson, Jerome's father (or grandfather, I discovered years later). Johnson's abiding commitment to the honkified NAACP was just part and parcel of his Oreo mentality. Mays liked to call a spade a spade, so to speak, wouldn't mince his words for a worthless slice of civic respectability. And black Laurel, like the civil rights movement years earlier, had divided along these contentious lines.

In Mr. Reid's eighth-grade American history class, Zeke and Jerome engaged in "rap sessions," as Reid referred to their frequent arguments. Black Power versus nonviolence, separatism versus assimilation, Fanon versus Gandhi, Malcolm versus Martin. Time and again, their rap sessions came to the same end: Zeke calling Jerome an Uncle Tom; Jerome calling Zeke an Uncle Tom; both calling their fathers and grandfathers Uncle Toms, followed by comments about mommas and grandmommas wearing army boots. Mr. Reid smoked his Lucky Strikes one after another, gazing on with a wide and agitated grin. Several times Jerome stormed out of the room in tears, though not before sweeping his hand against his brow in a stirring gesture of anguish. I sat flabbergasted, like the rest of the white kids in class. It was as if we were finally caught red-handed with our stolen notions of power—that our race and genealogy were in every way incomparable to the other's, that the dense computations of our blood and kin exempted us somehow from the greater human lineage. I thought, man, these black guys are intense. I couldn't keep track of their territorial disputes over authority—though I gathered that being called an "Uncle Tom" was serious business—but I thought it was all a heck of lot more interesting than anything I'd ever learned in the classrooms of Mason Elementary.

When school let out in the afternoon, Jerome and Zeke went their separate ways, and I went mine. I never thought of meeting them later in the day to play basketball or go to church. We were resigned, at least for a while, to the structures placed upon us, and this perplexed me at times (why— someone please tell me!—can't Joe come over and shoot hoops?), and yet more often the still divided social world was just part of the air we breathed, like Masonite's stench, life as we knew it. Exceptions to the rule, however, did not always suffer as a result. Claudelle Mays, Zeke's older brother, dated a white girl from my neighborhood. Claudelle shared his brother's irascibility without his interest in books or sports or politics. His only concern was a thirteen-year-old white girl who wore hot pants so snug you could see the soft impress of her genitalia. One afternoon I surprised the two in the woods while I was taking a shortcut to Old Bay Springs Road. They were sitting on a fallen tree smoking cigarettes. When Claudelle saw me, he narrowed his eyes and hissed, "Get the fuck out of here, white boy!" During pep rallies, Claudelle and the girl reclined on the back row of the bleachers making out. No one objected to the romance, which was obviously well on the way to all the way. No one dared.

Within a year, after the novelty of being together wore off, most of us settled down to everyday concerns, to petty disputes and aggravations, to periods of friendliness and toleration. Zeke Mays might even drag out a monotonic "What's happening?" if he saw me at the movies. I'd stand paralyzed with fear—even here he spoke with a clenched jaw—but do my best to choke out, "Not much, man." But our toleration was not the mellow embrace of the Coca-Cola commercials— red, yellow, black, and white hold hands in sunny meadows. It was more on the order of coming to see you as just another kid in the school.

Take Eddie Poole, for example, or more specifically his head, which resembled the shape of an ax. I'd noticed this myself but not thought much about it until I heard the black boys calling him "hatchet-head Ed." I took to calling him "hatchet-head" too, if I sat behind him in assembly. It wasn't racial hatred—or a sudden interest in phrenology—that inspired me, but the roaring approval of his black friends. Toleration might mean I've come to see you as just another kid to bully—as in Zeke telling me my breath smelled like cat shit or telling Whacker D. his pecker was too big.

Whacker D. was the name we gave to Chuck Yount, a skinny, pimply white boy who giggled incessantly. I don't know why we called him Whacker D. He didn't whack, at least not in the shower, and there was no D in his name. But it seemed to fit him just the same. The first time he undressed, everyone in the locker room went slack-jaw with awe. We all wagged our own penises in jealous mockery while he laughed nervously, without any hint of justifiable pride. The football and basketball coaches, the industrial arts teacher, a guidance counselor from the main building, people we'd never seen, stopped by for a look.

Zeke called Whacker D. a freak. Told him to take the thing on the road, join the circus. Or shove it in his mouth so he wouldn't have to smell his breath. Smelled like cat shit. Chuck broke down in tears. He'd cover himself with a towel whenever Zeke was around and turn his back on us in the shower.

The white kids in the locker room felt bad about the way Zeke treated Chuck, but we gave the boys all the room they needed. I sure wasn't saying anything, as mean as Zeke was. But one afternoon, Zeke's little routine came to an end. And the strange thing was, he not only stopped making fun of Chuck but even started helping him strap on his shoulder pads or tape up his ankle for place-kicking. Nobody could figure it out, but the bullying never happened again.

Years later I learned why. Joe Porter had taken Chuck aside one day and asked if Zeke was giving him a hard time. When Chuck nodded, Joe told him not to worry any more—he'd take care of it. And he did. During recess, Joe got Zeke alone in the boy's bathroom, grabbed him by the collar, and told him he was hurting the team and had better stop. Joe said he didn't know whether Zeke was picking on Chuck because he was jealous or because he just didn't like him. Either way, Joe said, the next time Zeke messed with Chuck, he would personally knock his lights out. Then—to show him he meant it—Joe pulled back his beautiful black arm and punched Zeke in the stomach so hard he doubled over in pain. Joe then waited while Zeke collected himself, helped him get back on his feet, and said, "I'm sorry to do that, but you asked for it."

All things considered, the civil rights movement could now be called a success. Free at last, you might say, the long arch of the universe touching down in the unlikely hamlet of Laurel, Mississippi. Or, at least, that's how it seemed to me as I daily negotiated the perplexing convolutions of race, sex, and religion on my own little piece of earth in my small Southern town. Whites had decided to do some overcoming of their own, prodded along by trunkloads of legislation, mandates and courtroom brawls, and the threat of a vanished economy. In the evanescence of the year came justice, gasping for air but still standing.

I sometimes think of how much better the process could have gone. The brethren and I down at First Baptist could have shown the world something great, been a church for the ages. We could have fallen to our knees and cried, "Oh Lord, have mercy on our souls," risked everything for the beloved community. But it also could have been a whole lot worse.

Integration brought us out of our homes and into the same schools, playgrounds, and locker rooms. Integration showed us, just before the truth became a cliché, that we really were all alike. I mean, there were blacks who liked watermelon, and blacks who didn't; blacks who smelled bad, and blacks as fragrant as an Irish spring; blacks with big tools and blacks hung modestly; blacks who loved Jesus and blacks who didn't give a damn. Not all of my white classmates were thrilled to discover the exquisite variety of their presumed inferior. Many didn't even bother to, couldn't have cared less, though I didn't understand this sentiment at the time. Integration seemed pretty cool to me. And yet, in those last days of the Jim Crow South, all of us—sons and daughters of the participants in the struggle for and against civil rights, with decades of white supremacy ringing in our ears—went quite a distance, farther than most of us have come since.

My classmates and I were not simply or only the beneficiaries of the civil rights movement. We could have resisted in any number of large and small ways, the ways teenagers do. We didn't have to take the baton, but we took it. We didn't have to stick it out for the long haul, but we did. We never sat down at the Kress coffee counter in defiance of public accommodations laws, ceremoniously order a burger and fries as if we were asking for the Kingdom. But we showered together in locker rooms, tackled each other on playing fields, and slept on each other's shoulders during night rides home on the team bus. Tim Harvey's clean lateral to Joe Porter in the warm sun of an October afternoon seemed to me as full of grace as any freedom rally or demonstration. We didn't need, and didn't have, television to document the moment, newsbreaking certifications of our accomplishments. We needed only each other, boys on the outskirts of manhood, linked together by time and good luck and an aching desire to go the distance.

In 1973, my last summer in Laurel, I went to church camp in the pine forests of northern Mississippi. I was fifteen years old and had been to the camp a few times on weeklong retreats, but I'd never spent a summer on my own, as was the plan now. The first night, I lay awake long after the other boys had fallen asleep, the familiar worries rolling over me full and heavy. The two months ahead appeared to me as an eternity, and I was sure I'd have to sneak over to the Chuck Wagon and call my parents from the telephone in the food pantry, a humiliating concession to my fears that I had made before. But as I listened to the night sounds of the forest, I remembered the words of a song we'd sung earlier in the evening, with the sky ablaze over the amphitheater, the sunset orange and blue. *Through it all, love prevails, be not afraid.* Now, in the iron-hot center of a July midnight, my body bathed in sweat, I shivered in ecstasy. The crickets embraced my joy like heaven's choir. I surrendered to my bunk and slept, fully peaceful, fully alive.

Notes

Chapter 1

1. In 1970, with not enough Jewish families remaining in Laurel to support a synagogue, Knesseth Israel would be torn down and the furnishings and building materials donated to two Negro churches.

2. Cited in Elmo Howell, *Mississippi Home-Places: Notes on Literature and History* (Memphis: self-published, 1988), p. 112.

3. Lavish Laurel, *The New Orleans Times-Picayune*, Friday, August 23, 1996.

4. Clyde M. Narramore, *Young Only Once: Secrets of Fun and Success* (Grand Rapids, Mich.: Zonder von Publishing House, 1957), p. 36.

Chapter 2

1. John Lewis, interview with the author.

2. John Lewis, interview with the author.

3. John Dittmer, *Local People: The Struggle for Civil Rights in Mississippi* (Urbana and Chicago: University of Illinois Press, 1994), p. 58.

4. John Dittmer, *Local People*, p. 266.

5. Cited in John Dittmer, *Local People*, p. 266.

6. J. Edgar Hoover, *A Study of Communism* (New York: Holt, Rinehart and Winston, 1962), p. 169.

7. Cited in *Jackson Clarion-Ledger*, Joan Mulholland Private Papers.

8. Cited in *The Jackson Daily News*, January 23, 1964.

9. "The Christian Conservative Communique," Volume 1, No. 2, March 17, 1965; Paul Johnson Papers, University of Southern Mississippi.

10. Claude L. Weaver, cited in "Mississippi Notebook," *The Clarion Ledger*, March 31, 1965.

11. Cited in *The Citizen*, June 1961.

Chapter 4

1. Cited in Don Whitehead, *Attack on Terror: The FBI Against the Ku Klux Klan in Mississippi* (New York: Funk and Wagnalls, 1970), p. 4.

2. "Executive Lecture of March 1, 1964," cited in William H. McIlhany II, *Klandestine* (New Rochelle, N.Y.: Arlington House Publishers, 1975), p. 123.

3. Bowers, quoted in Thomas Tarrants and John Perkins, *He's My Brother: A Black Activist and a Former Klansman Tell Their Stories* (Grand Rapids, Mich.: Chosen Books, 1994), p. 78.

4. Bowers, cited in Kenneth O' Reilly, *Racial Matters: The FBI's Secret File on Black America, 1960–1972* (New York: Free Press, 1989), p. 161.

5. Bowers, cited in McIlhany, *Klandestine*, p. 135.

6. Sam Bowers, "Executive Lecture of March 1, 1964," cited in McIhleny, *Klandestine*, p. 135.

7. *First Baptist Church of Andalusia, Alabama, Bulletin*, October 13, 1966.

8. September 22, 1967.

9. Buck Persons, "Sex and Civil Rights: The True Selma Story." (Birmingham, Ala.: Esco Publishers, 1965), p. 9.

10. Cited in George D. Kelsey, *Social Ethics Among Southern Baptists, 1917–1969* (Metuchen, N.J.: Scarecrow Press, 1972), pp. 251–252.

11. "Proceedings of the Southern Baptist Convention of 1954," Historical Commission of the Southern Baptist Convention, Nashville, Tennessee, p. 56.

12. Charles Robert Marsh, "Objectives for Adult Christian Education Implied in Paul's Concept of the Nature of Man," unpublished dissertation, 1966, New Orleans Baptist Theological Seminary, pp. 97–98.

Chapter 5

1. Frank H. Richardson, *For Boys Only: The Doctor Discusses the Mysteries of Manhood* (Atlanta: Tupper and Love, 1952), p. 10.

2. Frank H. Richardson, *For Boys Only*, p. 8.

3. Frank H. Richardson, *For Boys Only*, p. 41.

4. David Wilkerson, cited in Paul Boyer, *When Time Shall Be No More: Prophecy Belief in Modern American Culture* (Cambridge: Harvard University Press, 1992), p. 234.

5. David Wilkerson, cited in Paul Boyer, *When Time Shall Be No More*, p. 246.

6. The "frantic center" comes from Harold Bloom's terrific analysis of Southern Baptist piety in *The American Religion: The Emergence of the Post-Christian Nation* (New York: Simon and Schuster, 1992).

7. Lillian Smith, *Killers of the Dream* (New York: W. W. Norton, 1949), p. 85.

8. Lillian Smith, *Killers of the Dream*, p. 85.

9. Lillian Smith, *Killers of the Dream*, p. 85.

10. Jill Renich, *Preparing Children for Marriage* (Grand Rapids, Mich.: Zondervan Publishing House, 1964), pp. 20–21.

11. William W. Orr, "God's Answer to Young People's Problems: A Handbook of Christian Conduct" (Wheaton, Ill.: Scripture Press, n.d.), p. 42.

12. "The Home" (self-published pamphlet, n.d.).

13. Clyde M. Narramore, *Young Only Once: Secrets of Fun and Success* (Grand Rapids, Mich.: Zondervan Publishing House, 1957), p. 141.

14. "The Home," p. 27.

15. Jill Renich, *Preparing Children for Marriage*, p. 21.

16. "The Home," p. 42.

Chapter 6

1. Elizabeth Spencer, *Landscape of the Heart* (New York: Random House, 1998).

2. G. T. Gillespie, "A Christian View of Segregation" (Winona, Miss.: Association of Citizens' Council of Mississippi), p. 3.

3. Elizabeth Spencer, *Landscape of the Heart*, p. 161.

4. Elizabeth Spencer, *Landscape of the Heart*, p. 164.

Chapter 7

1. James Wood, *The Broken Estate: Essays on Literature and Belief* (New York: Random House, 1999), p. 249.

Chapter 8

1. John Dittmer, *Local People*, p. 2.

2. John Dittmer, *Local People*, p. 2.

Chapter 9

1. Cited in Stephan Thernstrom and Abigail Thernstrom, *America in Black and White: One Nation, Indivisible* (New York: Simon and Schuster, 1997), p. 167.

2. Cited in Seth Cagin and Philip Dray, *We Are Not Afraid: The Story of Goodman, Schwerner, and Chaney and the Civil Rights Campaign for Mississippi* (New York: Macmillan, 1988), p. 295.

3. Cited in Taylor Branch, *Pillar of Fire: America in the King Years, 1963–1965* (New York: Simon & Schuster, 1998), p.247

4. Cited in Seth Cogin and Philip Dray, *We Are Not Afraid: The Story of Goodman, Schwerner, and Chaney and the Civil Rights Campaign for Mississippi* (New York: Macmillan, 1988), p. 223.

5. Seth Cagin and Philip Dray, *We Are Not Afraid*, p. 441.

6. Erle Johnston, *Mississippi's Defiant Years, 1953–1973* (Forest, Miss.: Lake Harbor Publishers, 1990), p. 281.

7. On December 10, 1964, during a routine hearing in which government prosecutors attempted to send the Neshoba case on to a grand jury, the U.S. Commissioner for the Southern District of Mississippi, Esther Carter, threw out all murder charges. The Klansmen were photographed laughing and slapping each other on the back as they left the courtroom.

8. *Laurel Leader-Call*, October 17, 1967.

9. *Laurel Leader-Call*, October 17, 1967.

10. Cited in Florence Mars, *Witness in Philadelphia* (Baton Rouge: Louisiana State University Press, 1977), p. 257.

11. Seth Cagin and Philip Dray, *We Are Not Afraid*, p. 447.

12. Bowers, cited in William McIhleny, *Klandestine*, p. 209.

13. Cited in Don Whitehead, *Attack on Terror*, p. 211.

14. Cited in Don Whitehead, *Attack on Terror*, p. 213.

15. Cited in Seth Cagin and Philip Dray, *We Are Not Afraid*, p. 446.

16. Cited in Kenneth O'Reilly, *Racial Matters*, p. 176.

17. Cited in Jack Nelson, *Terror in the Night: The Klan's Campaign Against the Jews* (New York: Simon and Schuster, 1993), p. 65.

18. The same week, bombs detonated on the front porch of a Jackson parsonage while the husband and wife and their six-month-old son slept upstairs. The explosion blew shards of glass on the sleeping baby's face, but the child survived without cuts or bruises, as did Pastor Kochtitzky and his wife. The pastor, with help from Johnson, had organized a series of interracial breakfasts in Jackson. A Citizens' Council publication had described the Kochtitzky home on Poplar Street as a base of revolutionary operations frequented by Stokely Carmichael and Bobby Kennedy.

19. W. O. "Chet" Dillard, *Clearburning* (Jackson, Miss.: Lawyers Publishing, 1992), p. 165.

20. *Laurel Leader-Call*, November 15, 1967.

21. *Laurel Leader-Call*, December 1, 1967.

22. Allen Johnson, cited in Mississippi State Sovereignty Commission report, Mississippi Department of Archives and History.

23. The FBI's investigations into the White Knights' role in the April 4 assassination came to nothing, even though it was widely known among Southern terrorists that Bowers had ordered an assassination of King on at least two earlier occasions. At a fund-raising rally for the White Christian Protective and Legal Defense Fund at the Laurel Fairgrounds, Bowers's loony sycophant, Byron de la Beckwith, had urged the crowd of 300 to "start at the top and work down killing them." "The only time to be calm is when you pull the trigger," he added for emphasis. In 1965, Bowers had learned that Dr. King would be traveling through Mississippi between Philadelphia and Meridian, and made plans for his most ambitious "Project Four." But the FBI, acting on a tip from a Klan informant, averted the disaster by notifying King.

In 1967, a Klansman from Vicksburg named James L. Jones went to trial for the 1966 murder of Ben Chester White, a local Negro with no obvious ties to the civil rights movement. White had been shot seventeen times with a rifle and once with a shotgun. White's badly decomposed and headless body had been found floating in a creek near Natchez. Sam Bowers was implicated in the killing the following year, when White's relatives filed a $1-million lawsuit against members of the Klan. Three men were arrested on murder charges—Jones, Ernest Avants, and Claude Fuller—though Jones would turn state's evidence at a June 7, 1966, preliminary hearing when he testified that White was lured into the car on the pretense of helping look for a lost dog. Jones admitted to driving the car, but claimed he had not done the killing. Claude Fuller had fired seventeen shots into the sixty-five-year-old Negro's body. Avants had then shot White once in the head. During the 1967 trial, Jones told the court that White had been murdered as part of a plot to lure Martin Luther King, Jr., to Natchez where an assassination was planned. At the time of the murder, King was in Mississippi taking part in the Meredith March Against Fear, but he did not come to Natchez when White's body was found. *Laurel Leader-Call*, November 11, 1968.

Chapter 11

1. *New York Times*, January 26, 1968 (stringer).

2. Cited in Don Whitehead, *Attack on Terror*, pp. 254–255.

3. Cited in Don Whitehead, *Attack on Terror*, pp. 254–256.

4. Don Whitehead, *Attack on Terror*, p. 256.

5. Martin Luther King, Jr., "Letter from Birmingham City Jail," from *A Testament of Hope: The Essential Writings and Speeches of Martin Luther King, Jr.*, edited by James Melvin Washington (San Francisco: Harper, 1991) p. 295.

6. Based on testimony cited in James Silver, *The Closed Society*, (New York: Harcourt, Brace and World, 1964), p. 60.

7. Based on testimony cited in James Silver, *The Closed Society*, p. 60.

8. Don Whitehead, *Attack on Terror*, p. 256.

9. *Laurel Leader-Call*, March 12, 1968.

10. *Laurel Leader-Call*, March 14, 1968.

11. *Laurel Leader-Call*, July 26, 1968.

12. *Laurel-Leader Call*, March 21, 1968.

Chapter 12

1. Cited in Paulene Hester, *Our Heritage: A Foundation of Faith* (self-published), p. 138.

Chapter 13

1. See Robert S. Ellwood, *The Sixties Spiritual Awakening: American Religion Moving from Modern to Postmodern* (New Brunswick, N.J.: Rutgers University Press, 1994).

2. Francis Schaeffer, *The Church at the End of the Twentieth Century* (Downers Grove, Ill.: Intervarsity Press, 1978), p. 18.

3. Paulene Hester, *Our Heritage*, pp. 141–143.

4. Finch, cited in *Laurel Leader-Call*, April 4, 1968.

5. The *Hattiesburg American* reported the day after the bombing, "Members of several white families who live in the same general area

as the Dahmers said Dahmer and his family are well liked by both whites and Negroes in the neighborhood." "Negro's Home and Store Burned by Nightriders," January 10, 1966.

6. *Laurel Leader-Call*, July 25, 1968.

7. Cited in Don Whitehead, *Attack on Terror*, p. 247.

8. See the investigative reports by Jerry Mitchell in *The Clarion-Ledger* throughout the spring and summer of 1998, as well as his more recent series on the reopening of the Neshoba murders, "44 Days That Changed Mississippi," May 7–June 18, 2000.

9. Cited in Richard Aubrey McLemore and Nannie Pitts McLemore, *The History of the First Baptist Church* (Jackson, Miss.: Hederman Brothers, 1976), p. 262.

10. Sam Bowers, interview with the author.

Chapter 14

1. John Dittmer, *Local People*, p. 424.

2. John Dittmer, *Local People*, p. 425.

3. Cited in Adam Nossiter, *Of Long Memory* (Reading, Mass.: Addison-Wesley, 1994), p. 119.

4. See the story of Mae Bertha Carter and her seven children in Sunflower County in Constance Curry, *Silver Rights* (Chapel Hill, N.C.: Algonquin Books, 1995).

5. The plan was drafted under federal order by the Board of Trustees for the Laurel public schools in collaboration with the U.S. Department of Health, Education, and Welfare.

6. *Laurel Leader-Call*, September 2, 1970.

7. *The Citizen*, 1964, "The Kenneth Toler Papers," Mississippi State University.

8. John Dittmer, *Local People*, p. 424.

9. Tom P. Brady, *Black Monday* (Winona, Miss.: Association of Citizens' Council of Mississippi, 1954), p. 12.

10. Tom Brady, *Black Monday*, p. 74.

11. *Laurel Leader-Call*, September 1, 1970.

12. Conversation with Laurel attorney.

13. Cited in David J. Garrow, *Bearing the Cross: Martin Luther King and the Southern Christian Leadership Conference* (New York: Vintage, 1988), p. 481.

14. "Your Missionaries Speak," Historical Commission of the Southern Baptist Convention, Nashville, Tennessee.

15. William Martin, *A Prophet with Honor* (New York: William Morrow, 1991), p. 170.

16. William Martin, *A Prophet with Honor*, p. 170.

17. "Desegregated Schools Open Doors in the South," United Press International, August 31, 1970.

Acknowledgments

During the writing of this book, many people showed kindness when kindness was needed, and I wish to thank Carol Mann, my agent, for believing in the story, and to her assistants, Christy Fletcher, Yumi Ota, and Lisa Gschwardnter, for steady support and encouragement. And also Don Fehr at Basic Books, a good friend since college, and only recently my editor, for his intelligent advice at every stage of the writing, and his assistant Rob Kirkpatrick for handling the details with good humor; Bess Garrett and Alan Jacobs, for their friendship and editorial wisdom; my research assistants, Peter Slade and Brian Wabler; and Chryssy Wilson, Paulene Hester, Fran Brown, M. G. Dudley, Van Gardner, Ann Wald, John Dittmer, Sid Levin, Cleveland Payne, Joe Porter, and Spencer Perkins (whose untimely death still rattles my soul). I also wish to thank the numerous people who shared their memories about the last days of Jim Crow, and the archivists and librarians at the following institutions: the Mississippi Baptist Historical Commission; the Lauren Rogers Museum and Library in Laurel, Mississippi; the McCain Library and Archives at the University of Southern Mississippi; the Jackson State University Library; the State Historical Society of Wisconsin; the Historical Commission of the Southern Baptist Convention in Nashville, and the Mississippi Department of Archives and History. Some names have been changed to protect people's privacy.

I am exceedingly grateful to my wife, Karen Wright Marsh, for her sharp literary judgments and her careful reading of the book, and for another adventure shared; and to our children, Henry, Will, and Nan, my little heroes.

Finally, I thank my parents, Bob and Myra Marsh, for the many lessons they have taught me about generosity and kindness. In some of the nation's most turbulent times, they held on tight to the Old Story and refused incivility the final word. I dedicate this book to them with love and gratitude.

Index

A Note About the Author

Charles Marsh was born in Mobile, Alabama, in 1958, and raised in Alabama and Mississippi. He is a professor of religious studies at the University of Virginia and director of the Project on Lived Theology, a research project that seeks to connect the academic study of theology with the everyday patterns and practices of religious communities. His previous books include *Reclaiming Dietrich Bonhoeffer: The Promise of His Theology* and *God's Long Summer: Stories of Faith and Civil Rights*, which won numerous literary prizes including the 1998 Grawemeyer Award in Religion. He lives with his wife and three children in Charlottesville, Virginia.

A Note on the Type

Rudolf Weiss designed this typeface in 1926 for the Bauer foundry of Frankfurt. Weiss is based on typefaces from the Italian Renaissance, and is one of the earliest contemporary serif types to have italics based on the chancery style of writing. The vertical strokes that are heavier at the top than at the bottom are unusual, and give Weiss a distinct beauty. Weiss is a legible text type and an elegant display face for headlines or titles. Weiss is a registered trademark of Bauer Types, S.A.

DATE DUE

GAYLORD		PRINTED IN U.S.A.